Human Rights and Terrorism in India

BY THE SAME AUTHOR

Ayodhya: Ram Temple and Hindu Rennaissance

The Ideology of India's Modern Right

Hindus Under Siege: The Way Out

Sri Lanka in Crisis: India's Options

Rama Setu: Symbol of National Unity

Economic Development and Reforms in India and China

Corruption and Corporate Governance in India: Satyam, Spectrum and Sundaram

Hindutva and National Renaissance

India's China Strategic Perspective

Virat Hindu Identity: Concept and its Power

Building the Sri Rama Temple in Ayodhya

2G Spectrum Scam

Terrorism in India

Human Rights and Terrorism in India

Subramanian Swamy, Ph.D. (Harvard)

Member of Parliament, India
Former Union Cabinet Minister for
Commerce, Law & Justice

HAR-ANAND
PUBLICATIONS PVT LTD

Published by Ashok Gosain and Ashish Gosain for
HAR-ANAND PUBLICATIONS PVT LTD
E-49/3, Okhla Industrial Area, Phase-II, New Delhi-110020
Tel: 41603490
E-mail: info@haranandbooks.com/haranand@rediffmail.com
Shop online at: www.haranandbooks.com

Printed in India at Aakash Press

Preface

India today faces a formidable challenge to its national security and integrity from a overt war with China in alliances with its two allies, Pakistan and Talibanized Afghanistan, which specialize in covert terror-driven subversion of democratic India. Never before such a formidable combination of covert and overt subversion has threatened India's geographical integrity and terrorize India's peace loving population through violence.

Violence to overawe a civilian population to attain political goals is terrorism. This violence is also a tool to dismember a nation. The concern in this study is how to, as Indians, deter terror and safeguard national integrity. In India we see the danger clearly—in Kashmir, Assam, Northeast, as earlier in Punjab. The dismemberment of India as the goal of Islamic terrorism, of Maoists violence, and of the rump LTTE's perfidy should no more be doubted. In 1998, Osama Bin Laden identified the USA, Israel and India as the main enemies of Islam and targets for their terrorism. In November 1999 in a rally in Peshawer, the "patron" of Lashkar-e-Taiba reaffirmed this target/goal for India. On 8 June 2007, in a cassette distributed in a mosque in Srinagar, the Al Qaeda further confirmed that for Islam, India as presently constituted ("Hindu-ruled") is their target for terrorist acts. Thus, as early as in 2006, India become the nation that suffered the most terror-related killings after Iraq! India has lost over 53,000 lives to terrorism, and nearly 550,000 injured in terror-related violent incidents since 1996. In contrast in all wars since 1947, India today has lost a total of about 9,000 lives in casualties of war. India is under a terrorist siege today, of Pakistan, Taliban controlled Afghanistan, ISIS and other Islamic religion based terrorists, and Northeast insurgents supported by China and we need now effective total solution not piecemeal Kneejerk *ad hoc* measures. We can no more allow the malady to fester and become terminally cancerous. Terrorism feeds on a people who feel no bonding as fellow nationals. Thus terrorism and secessionism go hand in hand to balkanize a nation. Is then a democratic India in danger of balkanization, without nationalism glue?

With the dismantling of the USSR into sixteen sovereign countries in 1991, and the balkanization of Yugoslavia into four in 1995, it is now clear that political ideology of strong personality rulers of the state *cannot by itself* create social cohesion and preserve national integrity. Nor, as we have seen, religion can itself be the glue to keep a people together as a nation, as demonstrated in Pakistan in 1971 and Indonesia recently. Ethnicity also cannot be a sufficient adhesive as shown by the prolonged conflicts in Nigeria. Common culture as in Sri Lanka has also proved to be inadequate to keep a people from separatist conflict.

Hence we need to ponder what has so far, and what will in the future keep India together as a nation. Paradoxically, despite India's impressive record of keeping its integrity intact, it has been long predicted in the West, from Winston Churchill to Richard Nixon, that since India is an "artificial union," a British colonial construct, it will disintegrate sooner or later, because the glue of imperial power had gone. Churchill had predicted that it would take three years from 1947, while Nixon felt that dismemberment could be induced from outside to disintegrate India into twenty countries. But India has survived all the Cassandras, and ever since the imposed Partition of 1947, Indian territory has not shrunk, even if every inch of it is *not yet* within its control. If at all, the geographical span of India has marginally increased with the merger of Sikkim in 1974.

It is the thesis of this study that to deter terror, India as a nation must foster a concept of identity. This identity must have reorganized human rights foundation. A strategy to deter terror with human rights secured then can be formulated. From a study of nations that have remain united, and contrasted with those which have disintegrated, it seems that the crucial element for national integrity is the concept of "who we are" our identity, that the people within a geo-political boundary accept. This concept, however, has to be nurtured, renewed, continually enriched, and given substance. Such a concept, however, *cannot be forced down the throats of a people* as USSR and Yugoslavia examples demonstrate or allow the concept to derail a society as it did in Hitler's Germany. At the same time, the concept cannot be amorphous, meaning all things to all people, and without a time-frame for its acceptance by the people constituting a nation.

Dr. Samuel Huntington, a Harvard professor, has recently published[1] a study (titled: *Who Are We?*), about the concept of the US as a nation and its viability. He argues that the US as a nation is rooted in the "American identity" which is constituted in two dimensions: *salience* and *substance*. *Salience* is the importance of one's national identity over other sub-national identities (of language, region, profession, etc.), while *substance* is what one thinks he or she has in common and that which distinguishes this commonality from other peoples. *He suggests that a people with both, a definite salience and rich substance, will remain a nation, while others will not.* Hence, Dr. Huntington argues, the US has remained a nation because salience over the last two and quarter centuries has been clearly defined and renewed. He thinks that the most recent renewal emerged out of the American sentiment against the terrorist atrocity on 11 September 2001 (now abbreviated as 9/11). The patriotic sentiment upsurged amongst the American people, dwarfing all other sub-national identities.

American identity is also sustained by the substance rooted in "American creed," or what in popular parlance is called the "American way." Paraphrasing Dr. Huntington, the "American

[1] See his *Who Are We? The Identity of Americans*, Harvard University Press, 2003.

creed" may be identified as: (i) Anglo-Protestant work ethic (such as sticking to contracts, punctuality, verbal promise as bond, honoring IOUs, etc.); (ii) Christianity—religious belief in God, in good being rewarded, and evil being punished by Him; (iii) English language; (iv) rule of law and equality before it; and (v) individualism and the pursuit of happiness. Dr. Huntington quotes a 1931 judgment of the Supreme Court in which the apex Court held that the US is a Christian nation, and hence he advocates that acceptance of that is part of the American creed.

Since Independence from colonial rule, in 1947 Indians have been grappling with the question of "who are we"? *This as-yet-conclusive and unanswered, question represents India's identity crisis.* The failure to date, to resolve this crisis, has not only confused the majority but confounded the minorities as well.

However, without a resolution of the crisis, which requires an explicit clear answer to this question, the majority will never understand how to relate to the legacy of the nation, and to the minorities. Minorities would understand how to adjust with the majority only if this identity crisis is resolved. In other words, the present dysfunctional perceptional mismatch in understanding who are we as a people, i.e. the salience and substance of the Indian identity, is behind most of the communal tension and inter-community distrust in the country. It also weakens India's integrity.

Unless we settle the question clearly, finally, unambiguously, and authoritatively as to who we are, Indians will flounder, flip-flop, and generally be devoid of healthy patriotism. These then are the core fundamentals of nation: to know the salience in our identity, through a correct perception of our history, and to restructure our society on the basis of the substance of our identity. To achieve such a reform, of course, requires a complete de-falsification of Indian history, rejecting that portion that has been deliberately contrived by British imperialists and their compradors, and thus correct the currently perceived linkages to our past, to recognize that we are one people of the common DNA, and indigenous to the Hindustan peninsula.

In India, the majority is the Hindu community that represents about 81 per cent of the total Indian population, while minorities are constituted by Muslims (13 per cent) and Christians (3 per cent). Sikhs, Jains, Buddhists, Parsis, and some other small religious groups, represent the remaining 3 per cent. Though these smaller groups are also considered minorities, but are really so close to the majority community in culture that they are considered as partners of Hindu society. Unlike Islam and Christianity, these minority religions are born as dissenting theologies of Hinduism. They share the core concepts with Hindus such as reincarnation, equality of all religions, and ability to meet God in this very life by penance. That some of them feel increasingly alienated from Hindu society nowadays is also the consequence of India's identity crisis.

The India of today would not have been in existence had the past attempts to divide Hindus succeeded. Over the last five centuries, there had been attempts to divide the Hindu community into castes and races which attempts if had been successful would have made India a Muslim or Christian majority nation. The religious tax "jazia" was one such instrument to make Hindu society capitulate and convert to Islam. Hindus bore it and by and large did not succumb to it. The fact that undivided India in 1947 was 75 per cent Hindu testifies to that. English language and mores were used by Christians to convert Hindus. But Hindus have used the same to modernize and consolidate themselves, and finally overthrow British imperialists.

In the early 20th century, a sinister attempt to divide the Hindu community on caste basis was made (in 1932) when the British imperialists offered the scheduled castes a separate electorate. But shrewdly understanding the conspiracy to divide India, Mahatma Gandhi by his fast unto death and Dr. Ambedkar, by his visionary rejection of separate electorate, foiled the attempt by the signing of the Poona Pact between the Congress Party of Mahatma Gandhi, and brilliant scholar Dr. Ambedkar.

But the possibility that such attempts at dividing India socially may be made again in the future cannot be ruled out. Segmentation, fragmentation, capitulation and finally balkanization have been part of the historical process in many countries to destroy national identity and thereby cause the political division of the nation itself.

For example, the majority-minority question has dogged India for the six decades since 1947. Paradoxically, the Hindus, despite being over 80 per cent, are suffering from a minority complex, because Hindus of today are being confused by others on whether the Republic of India founded in 1947 is a legatee of the ancient Hindu India, or a new nation altogether forged as a byproduct of British rule and a series of foreign invasions earlier. This confusion, as we noted earlier, is at the core of our identity crisis. *The confusion will, however, disappear if we decide which of these two we are:* (i) An indigenous people of an ancient nation of continuing unbroken civilization, or (ii) an artificial administrative byproduct of foreign invasion and colonialism.

Indian history books written by the British authors under the imperialist's patronage, and digested by the English-educated intellectuals in India, have sought to foist the second concept. They have made out that India is a fusion of foreign invaders, first the Dravidians, then the Aryans, and then others. The British, they argued, gave us a central government which India never before had. This has become the staple argument of terrorists today. Division of India has become their political goal. All this is, of course, bogus history as Dr. B.R. Ambedkar in his writings on Indian history has clearly shown.

Writing a research paper in 1916 titled "Castes in India: Their Mechanism, Genesis, and Development," for an Anthropology

Department seminar at the prestigious Columbia University in New York, Dr. Ambedkar stated:[2]

> I venture to say that there is no country that can rival the Indian Peninsula with respect to the unity of its culture. It has not only a geographical unity, but it has over and above all a deeper and much more fundamental unity—the indubitable cultural unity that cover the land from end to end.

Dr. Ambedkar said 90 years ago what is most relevant to say today. He understood and had the courage and erudition to say that the British had manipulated our history to suit their ends. Following Ambedkar thus, the identity of an Indian is constituted by his adherence to norms of Hindu civilization, acceptance of sanskrit as the ultimate link language, individualism in the pursuit of spiritual happiness, being committed to the equality of souls and the law of karma.

In 1947, the nation had no doubt inherited a host of dehumanizing features such as poverty, communal antagonisms, and human bondage of various kinds. Human capital in the form of dedicated, tested leadership and a heightened mass consciousness had been accumulated during the freedom struggle. But since then, because of the policies and programmes adopted by the government and the political culture of the parties in power, this human capital has now been largely depleted. The inherited dehumanizing features have become further entrenched. The moral fibre of Indian society thus is weaker today than it was in 1947. That is the biggest inducement for terrorists to attack at will.

A society based on *dharma* is, therefore, vitally needed at this moment in our history, because there is a dimension to the current national crisis—namely, the moral decay and the decline of character

2. *Indian Antiquary*, Vol. XVI, May 1917, p. 94.

in our society which, if not stemmed, will slowly poison to death our nation. This decay and decline is visible in every aspect of our life—politicians defecting for office and cash, bureaucrats taking bribes, teachers selling exam questions, students passing by cheating, businessmen adulterating products, lawyers cheating clients, doctors betraying their patients, etc.. To some extent such degeneration is there in every society, but the alarming aspect in India is the pace of this decay and the spread of it. Consequent to this decay is the wave of dangerous cynicism amongst the youth.

This moral decay has to be stemmed to safeguard India's integrity. A renaissance of values in society has to take place. How will this renaissance come about? And what shall be its instrument, on which is committed to an ideology and determined to implement an agenda for renaissance? And what are the items of this agenda?

Since becoming free of British imperialist rule in 1947, India's ideological space had been for six decades circumscribed by a Left-leaning secular pro-USSR framework, with very little room left in the mainstream of thought for any other significantly different ideological perspective. Because of a dominant government controlling the "commanding heights of the economy," ruled by a party that became increasingly authoritarian, any serious secular ideological challenge to this was crushed at the nascent stage. Even when the nation faced a grave economic crisis, as in 1991 to resolve which required dismantling of the oppressive regulatory economic system, could not have been possible successful had the USSR not disintegrated leaving the Communist and Congress Left orphaned. The Left sought to undermine and discredit the reforms. The author of this reform who dared to deviate more than necessary from the past, namely, Prime Minister Narasimha Rao, was disowned by his party and the Left, and then pilloried, defamed and criminally prosecuted till his heart gave out. Even in his last rites, he was not honoured which was Orchestrated by a cabal of Left minded Congresspersons. Instead he was made an example of, for others who doubted this framework of socialism.

The Left-leaning secular socialists now seem to have had their innings, and are unlikely to regain the centre stage. What remains today thus is an ideological mish mash. Unless a new ideological framework is designed and presented with clarity to the people, the present hybrid ideological *ad hocism* will continue. This confused state of affairs, however, cannot steer the nation to new heights and world power status. *The nation needs an electrifying idea to secure national integrity and combat the challenge of terrorism.* The rising new threat to the nation of terrorism abetted from abroad requires a nation with a virile mindset of national outlook, founded on a correct perception of our identity.

To research, propound, and propagate a new ideological framework that can unite the nation, make the people strive to global greatness and struggle for world power, we do believe that the individual can be and should be motivated by equipping him with fundamental concepts of his individual, social, and an overriding concept of national identity, and empowered by adequate education, to bring about national renaissance.

The ideological framework to achieve such a national renaissance, the following parameters are essential.

(a) The identity of India is manifested in the concept of Hindustan which means an ancient nation civilization of Hindus and those of other religions who proudly acknowledge that their ancestors are Hindus. Hence "Hindutva" or Hinduness is the overriding and core concept of Indian identity. Such a state is to be minimalist in regulatory interventions in social and economic matters, maximalist in the maintenance of law and order, in opposing, terrorism, and optimalist in providing the quality of life needs, while being politically accountable to the people in a democracy.

(b) A social ethos based on the concepts of trusteeship of wealth, philanthropy and voluntary group action is encouraged by religious sanction for the better distribution of income and for minimizing economic contradictions and deprivation.

(c) The key goal of the state is to empower the individual through a modern education that blends the essential concepts of spiritual commitment with material pursuits to enable the individual to be self-reliant and yet have strong character.

(d) The individual is persuaded by the state by incentives and not by coercion. The state will hence make no promise to the people without specifying the sacrifices to be made.

(e) India can make rapid economic progress to become a developed country only through a globally competitive economy that requires assured access to the markets and technological innovations.

(f) Such rapid progress would require a national security strategy for a peaceful environment which necessitates strong security ties with such of those democratic countries with which India has no intrinsic clash of interests.

These parameters define a perimeter of reconstruction of the Indian mindset and outlook, and hence is an enormous but essential task that we have to undertaken to do, outlined in another volume titled *Hindus Under Siege: The Way Out* (Har-Anand Publications).

The present work is devoted to the concept of deterrence of terrorism in this Indian context, harmonized with international norms of human rights. *Defining such a concept of deterrence for*

India is the main contribution of this study. The strategy of deterrence of terrorism in India is original, while the other chapters are based on existing studies on terrorism, for which this author has reviewed, liberally borrowed, and assimilated the already existing literature on terrorism.

But here I have relied substantively on the previous research of other scholars I have acknowledged it by citation. *The purpose of this book, however, is not for scholarship in the field of terrorism, but to propose on the basis of existing material a new policy prescription for deterrence against terrorism, that is appropriate and consistent with human rights for India.* In that perspective, this book is more comprehensive than the earlier edition, in concept, *Terrorism in India* published by Har-Anand Publications in 2008.

SUBRAMANIAN SWAMY
Member of Parliament

New Delhi
July 1, 2021

Contents

CHAPTER I

Introduction

1. WHAT IS TERRORISM?

Terrorism is an act of violence that target civilians to overawe a legally constituted government and the people in the pursuit of political or ideological aims. In 1992, the General Assembly's Declaration on Measures to Eliminate International Terrorism, set out in its resolution 49/60, stated that terrorism includes "criminal acts intended or calculated to provoke a state of terror in the general public, a group of persons or particular persons for political purposes" and that such acts "are in any circumstances unjustifiable, whatever the considerations of a political, philosophical, ideological, racial, ethnic, religious or other nature that may be invoked to justify them."

Ten years later, the UN Security Council, in its Resolution No. 1566 (2004), referred to terrorism as "criminal acts, including against civilians, committed with the intent to provoke a state of terror in the general public or in a group of persons or particular persons, intimidate a population or compel a Government or an international organization to do or to abstain from doing any act."

2. WHAT ARE HUMAN RIGHTS?

Human rights are universal – in other words, they belong inherently to all human beings – and are interdependent and indivisible. The full spectrum of human rights involves respect for, and protection and fulfillment of, civil, cultural, economic, political and social rights, as well as the right to development.

In 1948, the UN codified these rights in the *Universal Declaration of Human Rights (Annexure 1).* In the Indian Constitution adopted by the Constituent Assembly on November 26, 1949, this was codified as Fundamental Rights.

International human rights law is reflected in a number of core international human rights treaties and in customary international law. These treaties include a particular the 1966 International Covenant on Economic, Social and Cultural Rights, and the International Covenant on Civil and Political Rights and its two Optional Protocols. India has ratified these two Covenants during the Janata Government tenure (1977-79) but the Protocols which establish the procedures have not yet been.

3. DETERRENCE AND PROTECTING HUMAN RIGHTS

While we worry about the impact of counter-terrorism measures on human rights, terrorism has a direct impact on the enjoyment of a number of human rights, in particular the rights to life, liberty and physical integrity. The destructive impact of terrorism on human rights and security has been recognized at the United Nations, notably by the Security Council, the General Assembly, and the new Human Rights Council [the former Commission on Human Rights]. Specifically, Member States have set out that terrorism as that which:

* ...threatens the dignity and security of human beings everywhere, endangers or takes innocent lives, creates and environment that destroys the freedom from fear of the people, jeopardizes fundamental freedoms, and aims at the destruction of human rights;

* ...has an adverse effect on the establishment of the rule of law, undermines pluralistic civil society, aims at the destruction of the democratic bases of society, and destabilizes legitimately constituted Governments;
* ...has links with transnational organized crime, drug trafficking, money-laundering and trafficking in arms, as well as illegal transfers of nuclear, chemical and biological materials, and is linked to the consequent commission of serious crimes such as murder, extortion, kidnapping, assault, hostage-taking and robbery;

Thus, terrorism affects human rights *in three ways*. *First,* the terrorist attacks deprive citizens of their lives, limbs and properties and hence their human rights. *Second*, to combat these terrorists we place restrictions on human rights of the citizens such as on privacy, freedom of travel and association so the victims of attacks suffer both ways. *Third*, human rights questions are raised when the terrorist are apprehended, on such issues as torture, deprivation of human dignity, the rights to a free trial, on clemency from death penalty, etc..

We thus need a policy framework structured in four dimensions: 1. A clear cut statement of objectives, 2. Defining the priorities of these objectives, 3. A strategy to achieve the objectives, 4. Commitment of necessary human, financial, and infrastructural resources.

In a nutshell, a government has to have the right *to do what is sufficient, but reasonable, to combat terrorism while maintaining human rights with reasonable restrictions*. Such Laws that abridge fundamental rights for crimes of terrorism, such Unlawful Activities Act, can be made within reasonable restrictions on fundamental rights such as reversal of the burden of proof and tested for constitutionality by the Supreme Court. The nation has learnt the Human rights value of such reasonableness during the 20 months of the State of Emergency imposed by the Indira Gandhi led Government

INDIAN PERSPECTIVE

The hoary concept of Hindustan [coined originally as a *sandhi of two words* [*Hi from Himalaya and Indu from Indu Sagar*] thus originally comprised the presentday India, Iran, Pakistan, Bangladesh, Nepal and Afghanistan. Ironically even today the Chinese in their Official documents and public conversations refer to India in the same way as they have been for the last 2000 years—that is "Yinduh Guo" translated as Hindu Rashtra.

It may be recalled that Kaikey in Ramayana was from Iran and Gandhari in Mahabharata was from Afghanistan. These two areas were 100% Hindu land till Muhammad bin Qasim's Arab force of the Caliphate led by Umar attacked in Sindh in 711. But that attack was repulsed by the joint army of Gujarat, Maharashtra, and Andhra. The repulsed Turks then again arrived in force 275 years later, and thus began the continuous onslaught of the land of Akhand Hindustan and fractured it.

Despite thereafter while fighting valiantly to defend Dharma and Matrubhoomi during repeated Muslim invasions for over seven centuries, the Hindus lost Afghanistan in AD 987, Iran in 1011; and present day Pakistan (and Bangladesh) in 1947 to Muslims.

After 1947, a truncated India i.e., the Republic of India that is Bharat, has meekly seen genocide, and also eviction of Hindus by Islamic terrorists from the Muslim majority Kashmir valley districts, not to mention the earlier exodus or forcible conversion to Islam, of Hindus from Pakistan and Bangladesh.

The percentage of Hindus has thereby dropped from 40% in Kashmir valley to less than 1%, from 19% to 1.1% in Pakistan, and from 32% to 7% in Bangladesh circa 2011. Such religious cleansing in the name of Islam has largely gone reported internationally even by bleeding heart Human rights activists.

Hence, every Union and State governments separately and collectively has a duty to take effective counter-terrorism measures, to prevent and deter future terrorist attacks and to prosecute those that are responsible for carrying out such acts.

At the same time, the countering of terrorism poses grave challenges to the protection and promotion of human rights. As part of States' duty to protect individuals within their jurisdiction, all measures taken to combat terrorism must themselves also comply with States' obligations under the Indian Constitution, international law, and in particular international human rights, refugee and humanitarian law.

Today, the nation is being called upon to resolve the conflicting demands of combating terrorism and of protecting human rights. The relationship between the two is not "linear", but is "non-linear". That is, *it is not true* that the less we protect human rights, the more we can combat terrorism. The converse is also not true. There is therefore a "optimum combination", of measures to combat terrorism and the level of safeguards that ensure human rights. The law of diminishing return operates on this trade-off.

The current position in terms of principles of combating terrorism are codified by the UN Human Rights Commission vide its Resolution No. 8 of 2005 (Annexure 2). The question before us how in India we go about combating terrorism, in light of our international commitments, and protecting fundamental human rights.

The fundamental question is that since in India we are seriously affected by terrorist attacks, even more than in Iraq and Afghanistan today, is how to formulate a policy to deal with terrorism.

The cure we choose for terrorist attacks should not be worse in the long run than the consequences of these attacks just as was the Kandhahar IC-184 plane hijack has showed. *In that episode, the Vajpayee Government capitulated to free three deadly terrorists including Mohammed Azhar, all three being in jail in Jammu before the hijack. These three had been caught after several police person were killed in an encounter with them. All three after release by the Vajpayee government as quid pro quo of release of !C-184 passengers [minus one passenger whose throat was slit in front of newly wed wife], were flown by Special VIP IAF Plane to Kandhahar, and handed over to Taliban. All three went to Pok from Kandhahar [Gandhar in Mahabharata] and founded three terrorist organization against India.*

Terrorism in India worsened as a consequence of the deal made by the Vajpayee's meek government to release these three notorious terrorist in Indian jail for freeing the passengers and crew of the hijacked Indian Airlines flight, but ironically more innocent people have been killed in terrorist attacks since the release of the three terrorists Maulana Azhar, Umar Quershi and Zargar in exchange for 159 passengers and crew in the Kandhahar case.

These three (on reaching Pakistan after being freed in Kandhahar) set up Jaish-E-Mohammed, LeT and Al Mujahedin which continue their terrorist acts even today starting with the dastardly 26/11 atrocity, continuing to kill innocent Indian citizens with terrorists attacks on civilians.

As stated above, violence to overawe a civilian population murder and arson to attain political goals is terrorism. This violence is also a tool to dismember a nation but colluding with anti-national internal violent groups such as Naxalites and rump LTTE . The concern in this study is how to, as Indians, deter terror and safeguard national integrity. In India we see the danger clearly – in Kashmir, Assam, Northeast, as earlier in Punjab.

The dismemberment of India is without doubt is the goal of Islamic terrorism, of Maoists, Naxalite violence. In 1998, the now deceased Osama Bin Laden had identified the USA, Israel and India as the main enemies of Islam and targets for their terrorism.

In November 1999, in a rally in Peshawar, the "patron" of Lashkar-e-Taiba reaffirmed this target/goal. India is thus under a looming terrorist siege today, and we need an effective solution for that menace. Thus, terrorism implies secessionism as goal to balkanize a nation. But Is then democratic India in danger of balkanization?

With the dismemberment of Pakistan into two in 1971, dismantling of the USSR into sixteen sovereign countries in 1991, and the balkanization of Yugoslavia into four in 1995, it is now clear that neither political ideology of the rulers of the state, nor we have seen religion can by itself be the glue to keep a people together as a nation, as demonstrated in Pakistan in 1971, *cannot by itself* create social cohesion and preserve national integrity.. Ethnicity also cannot be a sufficient adhesive as shown by the prolonged conflicts in Nigeria.

Common culture as in Sri Lanka has also proved to be inadequate to keep a people from conflict.

Hence, we need to ponder as to what has so far, and what will in the future, keep India together as a nation. Indian territory has not shrunk even one inch since, even if every inch of Akhand Bharat is *not yet* within its control especially in Kashmir and Ladakh. The geographical span of India as in 1947 has in fact marginally increased with the merger of Sikkim in 1974. China and Pakistan have illegally occupied significant areas of Kashmir, Ladakh, and nibbled away in Arunachal.

It is the thesis of this study that to deter terror, India as a nation must first foster a concept of identity. A strategy to deter terror then can be formulated. From a study of nations that have remain united, and contrasted with those which have disintegrated, it seems that the crucial elements for national integrity is the concept of "who we are" that the people within a geo-political boundary accept. This concept, however, has to be nurtured, renewed, continually enriched, and given substance. Such a concept, however, cannot be forced down the throats of a people. At the same time, the concept cannot be amorphous, meaning all things to all people, and without a time-frame for its acceptance by the people constituting a nation.

Dr. Samuel Huntington, a Harvard professor, has recently published[1] a study (titled: *Who Are We?*), about the concept of the US as a nation and its viability. He argues that the US as a nation is rooted in the "American identity" which is constituted in two dimensions: *salience* and *substance*. *Silence* is the importance of one's national identity over other sub-national identities (of language, region, profession, etc.), which *substance*

[1]See his *Who Are We? The Identity of Americans,* Harvard University Press, 2003.

is what one thinks he or she has in common and that which distinguishes this commonality from other peoples. *H suggests that a people with both, a definite salience and rich substance, will remain a nation, while others will not.*

American identity is also sustained by the substance rooted in what in popular parlance is called the "American way" Paraphrasing Dr. Huntington, the "American way" may be identified as: (i) Anglo-Protestant work ethic (such as sticking to contracts, punctuality, verbal promise as bond, honoring IOUs, etc.); (ii) Christianity – religious belief in God, in good being rewarded, and evil being punished by Him; (iii) English language; (iv) rule of law and equality before it; and (v) individualism and the pursuit of happiness. Dr. Huntington quotes a 1931 judgment of the Supreme Court in which the apex Court held that the US is a Christian nation, and hence he advocates that acceptance of that is part of the American creed.

Since Independence from colonial rule, Indians in 1947 have been grappling with the questions of "who are we"? *This as-yet-unanswered question represents India's identity crisis.*

Unless we settle the question clearly, finally, unambiguously, and authoritatively as to who we are, Indians will flounder, flip-flop, and generally be devoid of healthy patriotism.

These then are the core fundamentals of nation: to know the *salience* in our identity, through a correct perception of our history, and to restructure our society on the basis of the *substance* of our identity.

To achieve such a reform, of course, requires a complete de-falsification of Indian history, rejecting that portion that has been deliberately contrived by British imperialists and their compradors, and to correct the currently perceived linkages to our past, to recognize that we are one people of the common DNA, and indigenous to the Hindustan and peninsula.

In India, the majority is the Hindu community that represents about 81 per cent of the total Indian population, while minorities are constituted by Muslims (13 per cent) and Christians (3 per cent). Sikhs, Jains, Buddhists, Parsis, and some other small religious groups, represent the remaining 3 per cent. Though these smaller groups are also considered minorities, but are really so close to the majority community in culture that they are considered as partners of Hindu society. They share the core concepts with Hindus such as reincarnation, equality of all religions, and ability to meet God in this very life by penance. That some of them feel increasingly alienated from Hindus society nowadays is also the consequence of India's identity crisis.

Over the last five centuries, there had been attempts to divide the Hindu community into casted and races which attempts if had been successful would have made India a Muslim or Christian majority nation. English language and mores were used by Christians to convert Hindus. But Hindus used the same to modernize and consolidate themselves, and finally overthrow British imperialists.

In the early 20th century, a sinister attempt to divide the Hindu community on caste basis was made (in 1932) when the British imperialist offered the scheduled castes a separate electorate. But shrewdly understanding the conspiracy to divide India, Mahatma Gandhi by his fast unto death and Dr. Ambedkar, by his visionary rejection of separate electorate, foiled the attempts by signing of the Poona Pact.

But the possibility that such attempts at dividing India socially maybe made again in the future cannot be ruled out.

Segmentation, fragmentation, capitulation and finally balkanization have been part of the historical process in many countries to destroy national identity and thereby cause the political division of the nation itself. Hindus of today are being confused by others on whether the Republic of India founded in 1947 is a legatee of the ancient Hindu India, or a new nation altogether forged as a byproduct of British rule and a series of foreign invasions earlier. This confusion, is at the core of our identity crisis. *The confusion will, however, disappear if we decide we are:* An indigenous people of an ancient nation of continuing unbroken civilization, or an artificial administrative by-product of foreign invasion and colonialism.

Writing a research paper in 1916 titled "Castes in India: Their Mechanism, Genesis, and Development," for an Anthropology Department seminar at the prestigious Columbia University in New York, Dr. Ambedkar stated that there is no country that can rival the Indian Peninsula with respect to the unity of its culture. It has not only a geographical unity, but it has over and above all a deeper and much more fundamental unity – the indubitable cultural unity that cover the land from end to end.[2]

Following Ambedkar thus, the identity of an Indian is constituted by thus adherence to norms of Hindus civilization, acceptance of Sanskrit as the ultimate link language, individualism in the pursuit of spiritual happiness, being committed to the equality of souls and the law of karma.

The ideological framework to achieve such a national renaissance, the following parameters are essential.

(a) The identity of India is manifested in the concept of

[2]*Indian Antiquary, Vol.XVI, May 1917, p.94*

Hindustan which means an ancient nation civilization of Hindus and those of other religions who proudly acknowledge that their ancestors are Hindus. Hence "Hindutva" or Hinduness is the overriding and core concept of Indian identity.

(b) A social ethos based on the concepts of trusteeship of wealth, philanthropy and voluntary group action is encouraged by religious sanction for the better distribution of income and for minimizing economic contradictions and deprivation.

(c) The key goal of the state is to empower the individual through a modern education that blends the essential concepts of spiritual commitment with material pursuits to enable the individual to be self-reliant and yet have strong character.

(d) The individual is persuaded by the state by incentives and not by coercion. The state will hence make no promise to the people without specifying the sacrifices to be made.

(e) The citizen must have a mindset to bond collectively with others in the nation. At present, generally the Indian has loyalty to the family but is apathetic to the community where he lives. The Indians does not easily acknowledge the accomplishment of others. He respects intellectual endeavor but not dignity of labour, and is more concerned with form than content in personal and professional discourse.

A society based on *dharma* is, therefore, vitally needed at this moment in our history, because there is a dimension to the current national crisis – namely, the moral decay and the decline of character in our society which, if not stemmed, will slowly poison to death our nation. This decay and decline is visible in every aspect of our life – politicians defecting for office and cash, bureaucrats taking bribes, teachers selling exam questions, students passing by cheating, businessmen adulterating products, lawyers cheating clients, doctors betraying their patients, etc.

A renaissance of values in society has to take place. How will this renaissance come about? And what shall be its instrument, on which is committed to an ideology and determined to implement and agenda for renaissance? And what are the items of this agenda?

The Left-leaning secular socialists now seem to have had their innings, and are unlikely to regain the centre stage. What remains today thus is an ideological mish mash. Till a new ideological framework is deigned and presented with clarity to the people, the present hybrid ideological *ad hocism*will continue. *The nation needs an electrifying idea to secure national integrity and combat the challenge of terrorism.*

These parameters define the Indian mindset and outlook, outlines in another volume titled *Hindus Under Siege: The Way Out* (Har-Anand Publications).

CHAPTER II

Definition and Dimensions of Terrorism

Defining terrorism is rather tricky, and really is an art. Hence no book on terrorism can be complete without an introductory chapter on the definition of terrorism. Media coverage of every terrorist incident over the years has further complicated the difficulties of defining terrorism because there is no distinction drawn in the media between pure acts of terrorists and terrorism as a phenomenon.

A commonly accepted definition of terrorism does not exist even amongst the various concerned anti-terrorism agencies across the globe. In the United States, for example, three of the main agencies have placed different emphasis on the phenomenon of terrorism as indicated in Table 1:

TABLE 1
Definitions of Terrorism Adopted by various U.S. Agencies

Agency	*Definition*
Department of Defense	The calculated use of unlawful violence to inculcate fear intended to coerce or to intimidate governments or societies in the pursuit of goals that are generally political, religious, or ideological.
FBI	{T}he unlawful use of force and violence against persons or property to intimidate or coerce a government, the civilian population, or any segment thereof, in furtherance of political or social objectives.
State Department	(P)remeditated, politically motivated violence perpetrated against noncombatant targets by subnational groups or clandestine agents, usually intended to influence an audience.

Source: Mark Burgess, *Terrorism: The Problem of Definition, Centre for Defence Information,* Washington D.C., August 2003.

The above-stated official American definitions hinge on three characteristics: the motive, the method, and the identity of the perpetrator. The attempt here, therefore, in the Indian context is to define terrorism based on the commonality of motives, the method, and identity of those who practice terror. Terrorism, thus, is to be seen in multidimensional perspective.

The five main dimensions of terrorism, we hold, are: *First,* terrorism is organized by groups and sometimes sponsored by States. Most nations have experienced terrorism by both—the state as well as by groups. In fact, groups using terrorism as an instrument cannot survive for long without direct or covert state patronage. The states permitting the use of their territory invariably do so because they are using such organized groups as surrogates to achieve their goals. This method was first attempted after World War II, and for four decades, by the Soviet Union. The motive was to create disorder to enable a Communist revolution or create a pliant state to the USSR.

Second, modern twenty-first century terrorism exploits the technologies afforded by globalization, its foot-soldiers are weaned in religious bigotry and hatred, and directly targets democracies as their natural enemies. Today, for example, the main Islamic terrorist groups identify US, Israel and India as their targets. While some States do sponsor terrorism to achieve political goals, the terrorist groups, on the other hand, use social, economic and religious grievances or causes as their motive force. *Al Qaida* and Osama bin Laden, for instance, justify their *jihadi* terrorism on the ground that the US is their main stumbling block in achieving the goal of unification of Muslims into one Darul Islam, or pure Islamic State. In India, terrorist violence is almost exclusively directed at the Hindus, and those others thought of being soft on Hindus, or 'Hinduized.'

Third, terrorism being essentially an instrument of the weak and few against the mighty and many, therefore, the targets of terrorists are usually innocents rather than directly the armed forces of the state. Nowhere was this more evident than in the 11 September 2001 attack on US establishment. Terrorists using civilian planes brought about destruction and death to thousands of innocent civilians by suicide as never before in the history of terrorism.

Fourth, since the weak use terrorism as an alternate to war as we know it, they do not follow any norms. While efforts have been made in the last hundred years to make war subject to more humane norms and conventions, terrorism has remained without any norms as the most inhuman weapon in the hands of the perpetrators. No norms can, of course, be negotiated with terrorists. Moreover, terrorists do not have identifiable bases, i.e. a return address, structured formal organizations, or ranks in formation. They can be free-lancers, flotsams and jetsams.

Fifth, terrorism impinges on national security since terrorists operate inside a nation with overt or covert, explicit or implicit, support from abroad. A country has national security if it does not have to sacrifice the its interests and legitimate aspirations of the people to avoid violent conflicts, and at the same time stands committed, and able, if so challenged, to defend these interests by war if necessary. National security requires thus a nation's determination to preserve certain interests *at all costs*. Foremost among such national interests are: nation's integrity, political independence, and fundamental political institutions. Thus, in India's case, national security policy must concern preserving the nation's territorial integrity, political independence, fundamental democratic institutions, and ancient cultural values. While prior to the end of Cold War every nation had emphasized external security, now internal security has become as important an aspect to national security concerns of the state because of the rise of terrorism. National security, therefore, encompasses both—external and internal.

For example, Pakistan represents an external and internal threat to India. The two nations have gone to war four times in the last six decades. Pakistan-sponsored terrorism affects India's integrity as a nation as well. Pakistan's policy-orientation today is motivated by a feeling of revenge arising from India's role in dividing Pakistan in the birth of Bangladesh in 1971. General Pervez Musharraf himself had referred to India's role in Bangladesh in the Agra Summit in 2001. The All Party Hurriyat Conference (APHC) secessionist Ahmedshah Geelani, who claims to represent the people of Jammu and Kashmiri, had earlier said much the same to the media: "If Indian soldiers could play a role in the birth of Bangladesh, what was wrong with Pakistani soldiers playing a role in the independence of Kashmir?"

This goal of wrecking India's integrity was first pursued by Pakistan in Punjab in the early 1980s. Pakistan sought the creation of an independent 'Khalistan' hoping not only to dismember India, but create buffer for Pakistan. But Pakistan failed in Punjab at a cost of nearly 25,000 Indian lives, including ultimately that of Mrs. Indira Gandhi. Having thus been in vain, Pakistan since 1989 has focused its energies on Kashmir and other border states of India with the same primary goal—to dismember India. Already about 40,000 have died, and nearly 500,000 Kashmiris (Hindus) have been driven out of the State of Jammu and Kashmir into refugee camps.

Definition of Terrorism in India

Based on the perception in the above five dimensions we venture to define terrorism as we experience it in India. In India, terrorism today is defined as premeditated politically motivated and/or religiously-inspired violence perpetrated against non-combatant target population, primarily those of Hindu faith, by clandestine agents to secure compliance by intimidation, to overawe the Hindu civilian population to do, or not to do, an act against their will and well-being.

Terrorism in India, formally *is a strategy of violence, which is Hindu-centric-and-focused, committed by the perpetrators to generate fear, disruption, and with ultimate aim to secure their nefarious objective of balkanization of the Indian nation, the rubbishing of its ancient civilization, secured through capitulation of the civilian law-abiding citizens.* This definition, while it is relevant to India specifically, is in broad conformity with the brief official definition used in US[3] which defines terrorism as: "Life threatening acts to coerce civilian population or influence policy of a government by intimidation and thus affect its conduct."

India has had chequered history of experiencing such Hindu-centric terrorism. The earliest terror tactics in modern India were deployed in Bengal in 1946, by extremist Muslim leaders, Suhrawady and Jinnah, to terrorize Hindus to give in on the demand for Pakistan. The Congress Party, claiming to represent the Hindus [who were then 75 per cent of the population of undivided India], capitulated and handed 25 per cent of the territory of India on a platter to Mohammed Ali Jinnah soon thereafter. This was how Pakistan was born in 1947. That terrorism was also the embryonic form of the monster of terrorism in India today. Things have not improved much since then.

According to Union Home Ministry's 2004-05 *Annual Report to Parliament*, of the 35 States of today's India, 29 are afflicted by terrorism! There are about 25 terrorist attacks per month in the

[3]U.S. Fed. Cr. Code Chapter 113B Part I of Title 18.

country sourced to elements and bases in Pakistan. According to credible international reviews, India experiences more terrorist incidents annually (3,500) and terrorist-related deaths (3,100) per year than any country other than Iraq! India is thus today a seriously terrorist challenged nation which has profound national security implications. Combating terrorism has, however, become extremely complicated and multidimensional, hence we need to understand it's nature and scope clearly before an effective strategy to deter terrorism can be formulated.

Terrorism Today

Although terrorism is certainly not a phenomenon observed in the twentieth century, there has been a paradigm change in its character since 1968, caused by three specific innovations of the 20th century. *First,* the invention of television with instant satellite relay which has suddenly given small unknown groups the possibility of a worldwide publicity campaign. Internet has raised that publicity potential manifold. The fact, that most terrorist incidents have taken place in the democratic states may in part be due to the availability of this instant publicity. Under an authoritarian regime, such as China, terrorists can be cut off from their media audience in the target country, thereby losing all the expected impact of their actions.

With the freely available media, small groups of terrorists can achieve heavy leverage against powerful opponents by focusing large publicity on politically small events. The impact is mostly psychological and meant for media coverage. But it has the desired effect of promoting fear, shock and awe in the civilian population.

Hence, democratic nations now need to formulate their counter-terrorist strategy keeping this fact in view, not by imposing unreasonable restrictions on democratic freedoms but without destroying the basic structure of democratic practice itself, prepare its citizenry to become hardened to terrorists' violence. Spiritual guidance is essential for this purpose.

Second, is the incredible sophistication of hand-held weapons, especially it's miniaturization, and proliferation that have enabled a small number of criminally minded persons to do great harm. The erstwhile Soviet Union was largely the suppliers of these weapons to terrorists starting with *AK-47*. In 1973, for example, the Italian police nabbed five Arab terrorists who were setting up *SA-7* missiles in a rented apartment four miles from Rome's *Leonardo da Vinci Airport*. These missiles were intended for use against an Israel civilian airliner. The *SA-7* is a Soviet heat-seeking, precision guided missile. It can be carried comfortably on a man's back and can destroy a plane at altitudes of up to 6,500 feet. United States intelligence sources reported that *SA-7* missiles have surfaced in almost all Arab countries and some African nations, including Mozambique. Libya had obtained from the USSR large quantities of *RPG-7* rockets which weigh under ten pounds, can be hand carried and can destroy a tank, a speaker's platform, or a limousine. In this connection, the IRA is known to have used *RPG-7* rockets against armoured British military vehicles and police installations. Today, terrorist organizations have interlocking arrangement for purchase of parts and spares of a variety of weapons. The LTTE in Sri Lanka had been able to assemble six small planes by shipping in parts from Al Qaeda assisted organizations world wide and in exchange for drug and gun running by the LTTE.

Third, easy communication through internet and cell/satellite phones enabled active cooperation and networking between various disparate terrorist groups. The pilgrims at *Lod Airport* in Tel Aviv, Israel, were massacred by Japanese Red Army (JRA) members acting for the Palestine Liberation Organization (PLO). The terrorists who raided the Vienna OPEC meeting were made up of elements from the Popular Front for the Liberation of Palestine (PFLP), a PLO group, and the Baader-Meinh of gang (Rote Armee Fraktion, RAF), the West German anarchist group.

Within India, the LTTE, PWG, ULFA, Naxalites, Nepal-linked Maoists, Al Qaeda are all coordinating their terrorist activities and training due to these communication and weapons technology. The ISI of Pakistan is engaged in assisting this enterprise to unravel India, and push it toward balkanization. Hence, a terror cartel and networking has emerged in India. A counter-terror strategy for India thus requires a holistic approach and a paradigm shift from the traditional law and order approach of providing more personnel and more sophisticated weapons.

In 2004, the report of the Washington D.C. based official National Counterterrorism Centre in its publication: *Chronology of Significant International Terrorism for 2004* has reported that "India suffered more significant acts of international terrorism than any other country in 2004." It was a wake up call to reality, but India is still in a dazed stated, unaware the looming danger of balkanization by terrorism.

A deterrence strategy will now have to be formulated for a pre-emption of terrorists acts, and annihilation of terrorist organization for safeguarding India's national integrity and security.

On June 27, 2021, the situation of potential terrorist threat from Islamic extremists back by their Pakistan patrons has remained the same, except the technology has become more sophisticated. On this day, Pakistan sent drones equipped with GPS to Jammu to provide cover to terrorists trained in Pakistani hideouts to terrorize the people of Jammu, where Hindus are in majority. Obviously the Modi Governments to soft peddle the Jammu and Kashmir genuine integration that began in August 2019, had been put on hold. But June 27, 2021 incident in a rude reminder that nothing is changed for India's national security.

However, the complete withdrawal of US troops by August 31, 2021 will probably, if not certainly, mean the defacto terrorist Taliban, will bond with Pakistan's terrorist friend, the ISI wing to Pakistan Army. Pakistan which has slowly become a launching pad for the Chinese PLA and Navy will then as a part of the "unholy trinity" become a formidable danger to India's national security.

Chapter III

Lessons from History

International terrorism began and proliferated in the late 1960s. Between 1960 and 1967 there was a high incidence of aerial hijackings of civilian aircraft and taking of passengers of hostages. Most of the incidents were, however, committed for private or personal reasons by persons seeking political asylum, escaping criminal process, evading family responsibilities, suffering from psychological disturbances, etc.

In 1968, aerial hijacking and the taking of hostages acquired a political colour. The Popular Front for the Liberation of Palestine (PFLP), a part of the PLO, began hijacking for political blackmail. It was initiated in April 1968 with the seizure of an El Al Israel airliner which was commandeered to Algiers.

The erstwhile Soviet Union, which patronized terrorism as "revolutionary" violence, became itself affected by politically motivated hijacking. Even then it continued to extend international support to those nation and organizations which had supported terror such as Syria, Iraq, Libya, and PLO. An informal terror network soon emerged.

The International Department of the Central Committee of the Communist Party of the Soviet Union, the Soviet Security Agency (KGB), and the Soviet Military Intelligence (GRU) played the major role in building and guiding this terror network. Of these three organs of the Soviet state, the Party's International Department, headed by Boris Ponomarev, had been the most important Soviet agency for mobilizing and facilitating support of terrorism. The Department consistently promoted widespread "revolutionary violence," even while taking care to project the illusory image that the Soviet Union was abiding by the "spirit of peaceful co-existence." Setting the tone for the real mission of the Department, Ponomarev declared in 1964:

> We understand our international duty as consisting in support for all the revolutionary, democratic movements of modern times.... We Soviet Communists call upon all the fraternal parties and all the revolutionary forces to close their ranks more tightly, to overcome all difficulties, to rally under the banner of Marxism-Leninism in the name of the triumph of the working class.

Ponomarev drew sustenance from *Das Kapital* wherein Karl Marx had opined: "Force (*Gewalt*) is the midwife of an old society which is pregnant with a new one." Writing in 1848, Marx expressed a strong belief in the necessity of political violence: "Only one means exists to shorten the bloody death pangs of the old society and the birth pangs of the new society—revolutionary violence."

To facilitate these activities, Joseph Stalin had established the Lenin Institute (also known as the Institute of Social Studies, the Institute of Social Sciences, or the International School of Marxism-Leninism), located in Moscow. It taught the art of terrorism in the name of "revolutionary violence."

In 1958, Khrushchev had gone further to found Patrice Lumumba Friendship University at Moscow, to serve as a base for the indoctrination and training potential young "freedom fighters" from the Third World who were not Communist Party members. Specialized training in terrorism was provided in Baku, Odessa, Simferopol, Tashkent, and in the suburbs of Moscow. At these locations the techniques of guerrilla warfare and other skills – including the use of explosives, mining of transportation routes, commando field tactics, and the combat capabilities of shoulder-fired rockets were taught.

For example, Soviet Union played a role in the establishment of the Solidarite and Aide et Amitie terrorist network in Paris. This net work connected illegal groups, among them being the Popular Revolutionary Vanguard (VPR) in Brazil, the Movement of the Revolutionary Left (MLR) in Uruguay and Chie, the Quebec Liberation Front (FLQ), and the African National Congress (ANC) in South Africa, as the new Communist doctrine.

This doctrine was based on Marx's other writings, and in the works of Lenin. Writing in 1906, Lenin had stated "no Marxist should consider partisan warfare (including political assassination) ... as abnormal and demoralizing." On the contrary, "terrorist partisan acts against representatives of the violent regime, are recommended." That is, terrorism was regarded by Lenin as a part of the "proletarian revolution," although he wanted it to be employed only under the direction of "the Party." On the other hand, Lenin condemned individual acts of terror i.e., outside Soviet control, as "infantile," or "isolated" political violence.[4]

Leon Trotsky unequivocally justified the resort to terrorism as a tactical tool of partisan warfare. While Trotsky had been disowned by Stalin, his endorsement of terror as an instrument of revolution remained embedded in Communist Party doctrine. The 2012-2015 happenings in Nandigram, in West Bengal, confirmed that terror is an integral part of Communist mindset anywhere and everywhere, reformist or doctrinaire.

[4]Ray Clive and Yonsh Alexander: *Terrorism: The Soviet Connection,* Crane Russak, New York, 1984.

From the first Marxist-Leninist revolution against Czarism—when more than a thousand terrorist acts were perpetrated in Transcaucasia alone—to August 1991, when the USSR pathetically unraveled, Moscow had controlled Soviet-assisted terrorist groups, and made them to follow a strict party-line. Even terrorist movements with less party discipline and control, including the New Left, and Trotskyists (working for the furtherance of international Communism but generally hostile to the Soviet Union) received support when it destabilized Soviet-targeted societies.

It was the folly of the Soviet Union in capturing Afghanistan in 1979, and its forced retreat in 1989, that this terrorism was turned on its head, and it took on a fanatic religious colour of *Islamic Fundamentalism*. To borrow Marx's terminology, Soviet inspired "revolutionary terror" gave birth to Islamic terror with the Soviet invasion of Afghanistan acting as midwife.

On 8 September 1972, on the agenda of the United Nations General Assembly: "Measures to Prevent Terrorism and other forms of Violence" which endanger or take innocent lives or jeopardize fundamental freedoms was included for discussions of the Sixth Committee of the United Nations. The Soviet representative surprised everyone when he stated: "Marxism-Leninism rejected international terrorism as a method of revolutionary action because it weakened the revolutionary movement and deflected the workers from the mass revolutionary struggle."

The Soviet spokesman at the UN further held that "experience of revolutionary and national liberation movements showed that the recognition of terrorism as the principal method of combat led to a division of forces and *diverted active militants from their real task.*" Obviously, this change of tone and stance came because in early 1972, the Soviet Union suffered two hijacking and hostage taking incidents.

The USSR, however, reiterated during the discussions that it supported "the legitimate struggle" of the Arab people of Palestine "for the restoration of their inalienable rights," and that their terrorist acts were "acceptable and beneficial to the cause," because they made the people of Israel pay "with their blood for the criminal policy of their rulers."

The Soviet Union thus had used the terminology "terrorist" mostly to describe acts by Western states, in repeated attempts to identify the West with oppression and terror and itself with "liberation."

The *Pravda* (meaning "The Truth"!), the Soviet Communist newspaper, reiterated that position, while reporting on the 1972 United Nations Session on Hostage-Taking, as follows:

> "The people's right to oppose colonial domination, foreign occupation and racist regimes ... has been recognized for some time and is enshrined in the UN charter and several other documents of international law.... It is necessary to make a distinction ... between the people's sacred struggle for liberation and criminal terrorist acts by individuals, groups and organizations which have nothing in common with this struggle."

Thus, the erstwhile Soviet Union had continued to patronize terrorism by injecting the deadly ambivalence into the fight against terrorism. Thereafter, terror grew in only democratic countries and remained muted and stunted in brutally dictatorial regimes. By the time the erstwhile Soviet Union had unraveled in 1991, the damage to the cause of fighting terrorism had been done. Today, the world has to pay a heavy price for Communism's convoluted and suffocating ideology regarding violence against civil society.

Origins of Islamic Terrorism

Afghanistan was liberated from Soviet occupation in 1989 by Afghan Islamic Mujahideen, with US weaponry and Pakistani territorial sanctuary. The consequences of the Soviet adventurism have been profound for the globe, and has completely transformed the polity of Pakistan, and pushed that nation to the brink of disaster.

Islam and *jihad* have now formed the nucleus of Pakistani army's working at the domestic level as well in external affair levels and that nation has become a haven and crucible for nurturing terrorists.[5]

Pakistan is a state that was *not* created by a freedom struggle. It was instead handed on a platter by the occupying British imperialists in undivided India, and a tired, capitulationist Congress Party whose leaders were ageing and in a hurry to occupy offices of government. This tiring of leaders had been proceeded by a mass struggle of the people led by Mahatma Gandhi, who however lost his moral authority substantially when he acquiesced in the Congress Party agreeing to the partition of India. Sages like Sri Aurobindo had warned against the creation of Pakistan, but to no avail. Jawaharlal Nehru was bent up becoming Prime Minister with British patronage. For him cost to the nation of his aspirations meant little as we clearly see later in the policies he pursued as Prime Minister. Pakistan was thus created on religious consideration. A Muslim majority nation was born by British perfidy and Congress Party's complicity.

The impetus to the role of religion in governance and politics in Pakistan came in 1956, *when the first Constitution was adopted formally declaring Pakistan an Islamic state*. Thus, Islamic

[5]See Ashutosh Misra, *Jihadi Influence in the Pakistani Army,* IDSA Draft Paper, 19 May 2006,

fundamentalism began germinating in Pakistan quite early in its infancy.

The first formal effort to legitimize the *mullahs* (religions preachers) in the Pakistani power structure was made by the military dictator General Yahya Khan in 1970. He wanted to put on the defensive the secular parties such as the Bangla Awami League led by Sheikh Mujibur Rehman (in East Pakistan). *With army's support, the religious parties even won 18 seats out of 300 seats in the National Assembly in the fateful 1970 elections.*

The Army further drifted into a nexus with religious elements when the Soviets invaded Afghanistan in 1979. *Madrassas* mushroomed and *Mujahideen* such as Gulbuddin Hekmatyar and Burhanuddin Rabbani began to spearhead on the call of Islam, the resistance to the Soviet forces in Afghanistan. They enjoyed sanctuary in Pakistan, and radicalized the border states of Pakistan, the consequences of which have not yet unfolded in that fragile nation. In the mid-1990s, the Taliban, with some encouragement from Benazir Bhutto as Prime Minister, came into being and developed roots in the army ranks and cantonments. The Army began to organize regular sermons by clerics including Mufti Saeed, Sufi Iqbal, and Tablighi Jamaat members. The officer cadres in the army soon began to show signs of sympathy for the *Jihadis*, to acquire legitimacy in their ranks as well as with the ISI.

It is this network of *Jihadis* with the army at several levels of ranks, and later with ISI's support, that has become a serious threat for India today, and a source of various assassination terrorist bids on Indian soil. One cannot be anymore certain that a future *coup d'etat* by the Army would not enthrone a *Jihadi* as the new dictator of Pakistan. The Army-*Jihadi*-ISI network would then become official, and formidable. This would be a most serious threat to India's national security, since Pakistan is already a nuclear weapons capable state. It is this looming threat that India needs to ponder and formulate a counter-strategy and a well-thought out contingency plan. India needs allies in this endeavour.

The Islamization of the Pakistani army had gained vigour and speed under General Zia who came to power in a military coup in 1977. The situation in neighbouring Afghanistan created by a foolish invasion by USSR two years later provided the catalyst for Islamic radicalization of Pakistan polity. Zia provided the Army with the motto of *Iman* (Faith), *Taqwa* (piety) and *Jihad e-Sabilliliah* (struggle in the service of Allah!). The Army thus got the image as the bulwark of Islam, as the crusading Army of Allah. Zia wore the mantle of a saviour and one who would enforce *Ummah*. However, the adverse impact this approach had on the Army high command was the tension it created between the "modern westernized professionals" and the *mujahideen*. The professional image of the force fast began to wane, and has continued ever since.

The foundation for Islamization of Pakistan was laid by the frequent military coups, and the lack of "grass roots" democracy. Military coups were witnessed from the birth of Pakistan. Many were unsuccessful: for example, the 1951 Rawalpindi case leading to the arrest of 13 army officers, the 1968 Agartal case, and 1973 Attock conspiracy case. The successful coups were of Ayub's (1953), Yahyakhan (1969), Zia ul Haq's (1977) and the 1999 coup of General Musharraf's. Future coups in Pakistan are likely to be religiously inspired.

Noted Pakistani watcher Stephen Cohen[6] opines that the officers reared in the Army in the Zia years have now reached high ranks, and more religiously conservative than their predecessors. He notes:

[6]Cohen, Stephen, *Idea of Pakistan*, 2005.

Pakistani officers have come to believe that the West has targeted the Islamic world and Pakistan in particular. Like many Islamists they think Muslims are subjected to discrimination and army oppressions throughout the world—in Palestine, Bosnia, the Philippines, Iraq, and Chechnya—simply because they are Muslims and despite their favourable view of the United States as land of opportunity, many believe that Washington favours Hindu India and thus is no longer and ally, but a strategic threat to Pakistan.

That is, Islamization was promoted in the Army to provide the "glue" to keep an Army cohesive and a foster a compliant stable society. But it has changed the theological orientation as well, to a religious hatred of the US and Christian, Jew and Israel, and Hindu and India. Pakistan has been caught in a cleft stick contradiction: *bodily a US client-state but mentally increasingly with the enemies of the US.* The failure to resolve this implicit contradiction will mean the rupture of Pakistani society and disintegration of Pakistan itself. Such a development would pose a great danger to US, India and Israel. *A joint strategy of US, India and Israel to deal with Pakistan's potential instability has become an imperative for all three nations.*

This contradiction will first tear apart the Pakistan Army itself. As Owen Bennett Jones[7] pertinently observes: at present, the top there is only a tiny percentage of officers with strong religious views. However, he says that the Army may face a split and a spark an Islamic revolution. Jones thus states: "Those in the Army who favour Islamic revolution may be in the minority but that may not matter. If it were ever faced with mass Islam-inspired street protests in Pakistan, the Army leadership could find itself facing an awkward dilemma. An order to fire on such a crowd could well be

[7] *Pakistan: Eye of the Storm.*

disobeyed by some of the men." Pakistan will then spin out of control.

Thus, the disturbing trend from the American, Israeli and Indian point of view is the significant Islamization of the main Pakistani instrument of state power, the Army of Pakistan.

The implications for India's national security lie in the convergence of interests amongst the *Jihadis*, the Army, ISI and Taliban on issues ranging nuclear proliferation, to terror groups, counterfeit money rackets, drug trafficking, and *jihad* in Kashmir. There is growing evidence of the nexus, between this convergence and the rise of terrorism in India.

In June 2005, the Jammu and Kashmir Liberation Front (JKLF) Chairman, Yasin Malik, said in a statement, ironically made to compliment Pakistan's Minister Sheikh Rashid, that: "Sheikh Ahmed Rashid had played "a great role" for Kashmir's liberation. He used to support the frontline *jihadis* from Kashmir but few know of his contribution."

India's Intelligence sources confirm that Rashid had rented his farmhouse in Pakistan occupied Kashmir (PoK) to the ISI which was being used by the Intelligence agency for harbouring militants that Malik had referred to. The PoK-based JKLF Chief Amanuallah Khan had also claimed: "We had a gentleman's agreement, an oral sort of agreement. I was given assurances that the ISI was all out for the independence of Jammu and Kashmir" [see Ashutosh Misra, *op.cit*].

But it will not be easy for President Musharaff to snap the Army-ISI-*Jihadi* nexus. On 27 March 2007, for example, *Jihadis* had ambushed 5 senior ISI officers who were on tour in Bajaur area of North Pakistan. All five were killed. It was a warning from the *Jihadis* to the ISI for listening to the then President Musharaff for neutralizing Taliban. This animosity has been intensified with the storming of the Lal Masjid in Islamabad, by the Pakistan Army.

Despite this looming danger, there, however, appears no change in Pakistan's intentions as regards J&K. The terrorist infrastructure in Pakistan, PoK and Northern Areas remain intact, and active support to terrorist groups operating in J&K continues unabated. Terrorist groups and their sister organizations in Pakistan and PoK earned goodwill and sympathy for their role in relief work in the wake of the earthquake of October 2005. Pakistan Government tacitly supported various terrorist organizations in their endeavours.

Statistics, however, show a decline in infiltration and terrorist violence since 2001 in J&K because of stiff counter-insurgency measures[8] by the Indian Army.

The terrorist infrastructure has however remained intact in Pakistan and PoK. There are reportedly 52 terrorist camps which are functional despite repeated claims made since 2006 to the contrary?[9] However, to add credibility to its claim of being a leading nation in the "Global War on Terrorism," Pakistan has continued with the policy of shifting and relocating the camps to reduce verifiability of its support to cross-border terrorism, and make its denial credible. Deniability claims of Pakistan, however repeatedly suffered serious blows and caused considerable embarrassment to the establishment. A Pakistani weekly [*The Herald*, Karachi, July 2005, p. 5] long ago carried a report revealing the existence of 13 camps in the vicinity of Mansera along with photographs. Eric Benn, a satellite imagery expert with The US Defence Intelligence Agency, has also opined that there was "70 per cent probability" that satellite images pointed to a militant camp near Balakot in NE Pakistan. Such satellite proof has been

[8]See Charts 1 and 2 and Tables 3 and 4 below Annexure I.

[9]E . Ahmed, Minister of State for External Affairs, *Statement made in response to Parliament Question*, no. 1192, in Lok Sabha on 2 August 2006.

produced by FBI in US courts as evidence against terrorists from Pakistan facing trial. Of course, in 2017, the BJP Government bombed these camps after producing photo/video proof of such camps.

Latest reports indicate existence of three camps in Mansera and Abbottabad districts, besides presence of thousands of militants of Lashkar-e-Taiba (LeT), Jaish-e-Mohammed (JeM). Harkat-ul-Mujahideen (HuM), Al Badr, Hizb-ul-Mujahideen and other smaller Tanzeems in Frontier and PoK regions. The catch-22 situation the West found itself in both needing Pakistan to deal with terrorism in Afghanistan especially of Al Qaeda, and requiring to humour Pakistan's propensity to promote terror across its borders had encouraged Pakistan to continue maintaining the terrorist infrastructure to destabilize Jammu and Kashmir.

In October 2005 earthquake, the terrorist infrastructure in PoK did suffer damages; however, the same has been taken care of. The earthquake provided an opportunity to Tanzeems to earn the goodwill and sympathy of the local populace by doing relief work. Jamaat-ud-Daawa (JuD), the parent organization of LeT, was the main beneficiary. Shiv Shankar Menon, the then Indian High Commissioner to Pakistan (later National Security Advisor) had said, "The involvement of terrorist organizations in relief work after the earthquake had resulted in their public rehabilitation. Renewed goodwill for Tanzeems and availability of charity funds post- earthquake, combined with availability of unemployed youths, has strengthened terrorist support base and infrastructure in PoK."

Unfortunately, for India's national security, parallel to these developments within Pakistan, an Islamic radicalization was also developed in Kashmir, perhaps unwittingly by the Congress-National Conference alliance in the 1980s; the pandering for votes that saw the rise of such movements as *the Jammu and Kashmir Liberation Front, Mahaz-i-Azadi* and the *Liberation League.*

By 1985, both the *Jamaat-i-Islami* and *Al Jihad* movements, the latter a clandestine organization influenced by the ideology of the Iranian revolution, were becoming highly influential in Kashmiri politics. Indeed, the *Al Jihad* movement publicly raised the issue of an Islamic Revolution as the only way to liberate Kashmir in the mid-1980s. Thus, in the space of a few short years, there was a marked erosion of the *Kashmiriyat*, which historically meant a mildly secular personality of the people of the state. Instead a Muslim identity with fundamentalist overtones started to emerge in the state.

This transformation was initially assisted and reinforced by an active ISI programme, by using the Afghan infrastructure in Pakistan. Indeed, during the main escalation of Islamist violence in Kashmir in mid-1988, Pakistan provided assistance in the training and arming of Kashmiri terrorists, as well as sanctuaries to Kashmiri insurgents across the border. Often this assistance was funnelled through the Afghan rebel leader Gulbadin Hikmatyar's *Hizb-e-Islami* group for deniability. Now in 2021, even the 'fig leaf' has become unnecessary.

With considerable growing experience in training, organizing and running the Afghan *mujahideen,* and with military supplies available (through US, Saudi and other foreign assistance), Pakistan began expanding its operation in mid-2010s to promote separatism and sponsor terrorism in Kashmir, as a strategic long-term programme of seeking to balkanize India, or at least keep the Indian nation hemorrhaging.

Thus the rise of Islamist ideology to predominance throughout Kashmir facilitated the emergence of a networking of terrorist activities, amongst Kashmiri militants, their logistical supporters and Pakistan. Moreover, with the increased terrorism in India, the ISI had been able to keep out the Afghani *mujahideen* from meddling in Pakistani domestic politics, and has been successful in that regard at least to date.

Sadly the first distinctive boost to terrorism in Kashmir was provided by Farooq Abdullah as Chief Minister when for his narrow political posturing he released terrorists from jail in May 1989, that led to genocide of Kashmiri Hindus, Sikhs and Buddhists, and a mass exodus of over 500,000 non-Muslims to other parts of India and the Western nations.

Within months, these released terrorists belonging to several militant groups emerged advocating *Nizam-e-Mustafa* as the objective of their struggle. *Azadi* gave way to *jihad*. Groups such as Jamaat-e-Islami and its militant wing, Hizbul Mujahideen, the radical women's wing, Dukhtaran-i-Millat, Jamiat-ul-Mujahideen, Allah Tigers, Jamiat-ul-Ulemma Islam, Al Badr, Al Jihad Force, Al Umar Mujahideen, Muslim Mujahideen, Islamic Students League, Zia Tigers, swore by Islamization, merger of Kashmir with Pakistan, unification of the *Ummah*, and finally establishment of an Islamic Caliphate as their objective. The proposed merger of Kashmir with Pakistan, which had little support amongst the broad masses of Kashmiris, was nevertheless propagated as a step towards the unification of Ummah. *Hizbul Mujahideen* asserted that its aim "is the establishment of Islamic Caliphate world over. We do not believe in ideological or geographical boundaries." Another group, Jamiat-ul-Mujahideen, stressed that "the demand for self-determination was distorting the image of the ongoing movement. It is a struggle for the establishment of Caliphate." The "Allah Tigers" claimed that, the present struggle would continue until the goal of establishing an Islamic Caliphate was achieved.

An immediate consequence of the cry for the unification of Ummah was the liquidation programme of central government officials, the uprooting of Kashmiri Pandits, the decimation by assassinations of nationalist Muslim intellectuals, terrorizing liberal activists, a sense-less programmes of genocide described as necessary by the terrorists to "cleanse" the valley of its "un-Islamic" elements. Cinema-houses, beauty parlours, wine shops, bars, video centres, use of cosmetics, etc. were declared as "banned." Al Barq, for example, issued a ban order on selling of even cigarettes. Another outfit, the Peoples League, demanded that Kashmiri girls not to take part in any cultural programmes outside the Valley. The Allah Tigers threatened to throw bombs on houses where women would refuse to wear veils. They even sought to coerce local newspapers to highlight their activities and play down national news activities. The Hizbul Mujahideen went a step further imposed a ban on the circulation of national and even Jammu newspapers in the Valley. This was "Talibanism" ahead ofTaliban regaining Afghanistan.

Thus, the Islamic hue of insurgency in Kashmir became more obvious with Hizbul Mujahideen, Jamiat-ul-Mujahideen, Harkat-ul-Ansar, Lashkar-e-Toiba and Markaz Dawa-ul-Irshad embarking on a religious "crusade" against the non-Muslim minorities in the state and publicly owning responsibility for killing Hindus in the name of *jihad.* Through a press release dated 14 April 1990, an ultimatum was given to the Hindu community, demanding that they leave the Valley "within two days" or face death. About 1,000 Hindus were brutally murdered as an example, and thereafter about 500,000 left the state to become refugees in their own country. This community is scattered in squalid camps in Jammu, Delhi and other parts of India. Moreover, nearly 30,000 houses belonging to Kashmiri Pandits, hundreds of their business establishments, educational, cultural and religious institutions have been either confiscated or destroyed. The objective was to rub out all traces of non-Muslim Kashmir culture, and the Islamic *jihadi* terrorists have almost accomplished their objective in a nation of 82 per cent Hindus. Indians cannot rest till these displayed Kashmiri non-Muslims are restored to their homes in Kashmir Valley.

Terrorists have recruited thousands of young Muslims of the Valley, since then and coerced them to cross the LAC (Line of Actual Control), to undergo training in weapons and explosives in various training camps set up in Pak-occupied Kashmir, Pakistan and Afghanistan. Those of local youth who resisted were kidnapped and even tortured, some killed. In this second phase of militancy, the local Muslims bore the brunt of atrocities by the terrorists and other mercenaries. A series of assassinations and bomb attacks on social and political activists belonging to nationalist and liberal sections of Muslim society in Kashmir were carried out to destroy established political institutions and to thwart democracy in the state. The Chief of Lashkar-e-Toiba, Hafiz Mohammad Khan, went on record to state: "Democracy is among the menaces we inherited.... These are all useless practices and part of the system we are fighting against. If God gives us a chance, we will try to bring in the pure concept of an Islamic Caliphate."

The possibility of establishing a new Islamic Caliphate running from Kashmir to Pakistan through Afghanistan and the new States of Central Asia was propagated by the Islamist terrorists to motivate the people of Kashmir. The leader of Jamaat-e-Islami (Pakistan) Qazi Hussain Ahmed, on the Kashmir Solidarity day in Rawalpindi in February 1992, had also declared that, "a great Islamic state, spreading from Kashmir to Central Asia would emerge after the independence of Kashmir."

But there was an unexpected consequence of this war cry. *Jihad,* though forged unity between the Afghan Mujahideen and Kashmiri militants, nevertheless caused the insurgency in Kashmir to lose its indigenous character which the JKLF had fostered. Islamic radicals, besides and Afghan and Pakistani mercenaries, have now emerged as leaders, alienating the local Kashmiri youth from the movement. Hence, the terrorist groups today engaged in Kashmir, including Harkat-ul-Mujahideen, are foreign-led, and products of the anti-Soviet Afghan struggle. The Taliban, moreover, is an important agent fuelling the fire of Islamic militancy in Kashmir.

Terrorism when blended with *jihad* is a deadly mix and a major challenge to national security and integrity of India. Had there been no '9/11' terrorist attack in US, and the consequent US-led conquest of Afghanistan, things would been much much worse for India today. As Masood Khalili, the Ambassador of Afghanistan in India, has observed in interview to a Delhi newspaper: "By end-2001, entire Afghanistan would have been captured by Taliban. By now, most of Uzbekistan, Tajikistan and Kyrgyzstan would have been run over by Al Qaeda. Afghanistan would have become a *Khilafat* (Caliphate), training and exporting 50,000 terrorists. The world would have had to recognize the Taliban, welcoming them to the OIC and the UN." With Al Qaeda at India's doorstep, what would have happened to J&K can easily be imagined. The Islamic terrorist epidemic has been contained for now, but the responsibility that devolves on India, to keep it that way, is heavy. It requires India to squarely face the implications of the almost lone battle that the US had faced is waging in Iraq and Afghanistan and now quit. This requires for India's civil society to be properly educated about the stakes involved and the nation's patriotic options. While we may pursue friendship with at the foreign policy level, effective national security policy calls for constant search for the vulnerability points of Pakistan and Bangladesh for future use for ending India directed terrorism.

A brief background about the Northern Areas is useful at this stage, since these areas are going to be vital in future anti-terrorist operations of India. The Northern Areas of Pakistan-occupied

Kashmir was annexed by Pakistan during 1947-48. [For a perceptive analysis of the region see *Dr. Alok Bansel* "Alienation in Northern Areas of PoK" IDSA papers, New Delhi, 2006]. Gilgit-Baltistan, as this region is referred to in local literature, came under Pakistani control, when Major Brown, the British Commander of Gilgit Scouts, an Indian Army unit, unauthorizedly declared accession to Pakistan on 4 November 1947. Soon the region was named "The Northern Areas of Pakistan" and was put under the direct control of Islamabad, separate from Pakistan-Administered "Azad (Independent) Kashmir." Unlike Pakistan's other four provinces, the Northern Areas have no political representation in the parliament or the federal cabinet and no status under Pakistan's constitution. Also, unlike the other parts of Pakistan-occupied Kashmir (PoK) called "Azad Kashmir" which has a modicum of self-governance; these areas are directly administered by Islamabad through a non-elected federal minister for Northern Areas.

The sparsely populated mountainous region has an area of 28,000 square miles, which makes it slightly smaller than North West Frontier Province (NWFP) and more than six times the size of "Azad Kashmir." Famous for its peaks, rivers, glaciers and exotic cultures, the region is divided into six districts of Gilgit, Skardu, Diamer, Ghizer, Ghanche and Astore. With the Karakoram, Himalaya and Hindukush ranges as a backdrop, the region shares borders with China, Jammu and Kashmir, Afghanistan and Chitral district of NWFP.

Overwhelming majority of the population of two million of the area believed to follow different schools of Shiaism. In the recent past, the schools in the region had to remain closed for almost a year because different sects could not agree on the contents of the textbooks. There have been numerous acts of violence where people have invariably targeted the symbols of government authority like police personnel and government officials. These are nothing but manifestation of people's alienation with the government. Recent statements by members of Gilgit Baltistan United Movement, where they have not only accused Indian government of not doing enough for them but have also demanded reservation in Indian educational institutions for the residents of Northern Areas (!), shows the level of their alienation with Pakistan.

The surrounding areas, which were in the immediate vicinity of the quake affected region, were engulfed in serious sectarian riots. At a time when public solidarity in Pakistan was reported to be comparable to the heady days of 1965, this region remained under curfew for weeks in the immediate aftermath of the quake and over a dozen lives were lost in clashes between Pakistani Rangers and Shia students.

Historically, Northern Areas evolved as two separate political entities: Dardistan [or Gilgit], and Baltistan. Though there were times when they were part of the same political entity, the two political entities were eventually united during the Sikh rule and remained so during the subsequent Dogra rule.

Dardic Gilgit, whose language Dardic has Sanskrit/Pali roots, is a region that was part of the Mauryan Empire. According to Dr. Ahmed Dani, Ashoka's fourteen rock edicts are still surviving along the Karakoram Highway [see his *History of Northern Areas of Pakistan* (1991)]. Subsequently, the region was conquered by the Kushanas and, on their subsequent decline, by the Huns. During 6th to 8th centuries, Gilgit was the home of the Patola rulers, who practiced Buddhism and had interactions with the rulers of Kashmir and the emperors of China. Apart from Kashmiri influence, the Tibetans also have influenced the culture of area.

Geopolitically, it is one of political and strategic importance with the opening of the Karakoram Highway, which links China to Pakistan and reportedly generates trade worth billions of dollars. The region, however, has become the stage for violent protests by the impoverished population of Northern Areas, which believes that their unique ethno-cultural and religious identity is being threatened. The alienation of the populace in Northern Areas is increasing and besides ethnicity has a strong sectarian undertone. Northern Areas territory is, thus, emerging as an "Achilees Heel" of Pakistani defence of Kashmir.

The acts of violence in Gilgit area are indicative of the damage being done to Northern Areas in the absence of any genuine democratic and constitutional mechanism to solve their problems. The continued denial of a say in the governance of the region and unabashed exploitation of the resources of the region without showing any concern for its harmful effects on the local population has led to severe estrangement of the population with the ruling elite in Islamabad. Such announcements have naturally caused widespread anger in the region and has increased the alienation of the population but the feelings and aspirations of the people of Northern Areas have never mattered to the ruling elite in Islamabad, which often treats the region as a colony. Pakistani elite, which habitually complain about the alleged violation of human rights in Jammu and Kashmir, rarely raise a voice in support of the exploited population of the Northern Areas. In the Pakistani scheme of things, the Northern Areas have an extremely ambiguous constitutional position and its status has never been defined in international law. It is neither a province of Pakistan nor a sovereign state; it is just a "local authority" to manage territory occupied by Pakistan. In fact, since its accession to Pakistan, the people have been denied the right to vote for their own representatives and have been governed by administrators from Islamabad.

The frequent sectarian violence triggered in Northern Areas has continued to rock the region that was once known for its tranquillity. Even the vital Karakoram Highway linking Pakistan to

China was sometimes blocked. The spontaneous reaction to the killings was indicative of the simmering discontent within the populace of Northern Areas. Government officials, including those of Army, Northern Light Infantry and police, have been identified and murdered while travelling in buses in areas falling under the control of rival sects.

Gilgit was founded in 1842 by Syed Nathe Shah, the commander of Sheikh Ghulam Mohi-ud-din, the governor appointed by Sikhs of Kashmir. Early history of Baltistan begins with the spread of Buddhism under the Kushans. Makpon Bokha is said to have founded the State of Baltistan in about 15th century A.D. He also made an administrative seat and palace at Kharpoche and built a fort there.

After conquering Ladakh in 1836, the Dogras turned towards Baltistan and in 1840 Dogra General Zorawar Singh leading a contingent of Dogra and Ladakhi troops conquered Baltistan and installed a puppet ruler. Zorawar Singh returned to Leh after stationing a garrison at Skardu. Thus, Baltistan became part of Dogra kingdom much before Kashmir Valley and Gilgit.

The British defeated the Sikhs due to the treachery of Raja Gulab Singh, he was handed over all the territories of the Punjab State situated east of river Indus and West of river Ravi. Raja Gulab Singh occupied Kashmir in October 1846. Subsequently, with the signing of Treaty of Amritsar in 1846, the British encouraged Gulab Singh to spread his political influence in the Northern Areas so as to establish a safe buffer state between Russia and British India. By 1866, the entire region had come under the control of the Dogras and the rulers of Hunza and Nagar became vassals of Kashmir.

Consequent to the Russian revolution in 1917, the British anxieties over the region increased and the Maharaja was forced to lease the Gilgit Agency to the British for 60 years on 26 March 1935. This has expired on 27 March 1995, and hence by the Instrument of Accession signed by the Maharaja of J&K, Northern Areas, or Gilgit-Baltistan as it should be known, has merged with India fully and formally. The agreement had given the Viceroy the right to assume civil and military administration of the Wazarat of Gilgit Province that lay beyond the right bank of river Indus. Maharaja was then in no position to resist the British pressure. As a result, despite being a part of Maharaja's territory, Gilgit and surrounding regions of Dardistan including the vassal states were virtually administered by the British directly from 1935 to 1947. Though a modicum of Maharaja's authority was maintained by way of flying his flag at the official headquarters of the agency and by way of appointment of certain state officials in Gilgit, the only real authority with the Maharaja was to grant mining licences and leases. However, all the area to the left of river Indus in Dardistan and the entire Baltistan remained under the direct control of Maharaja. The announcement of Independence in 1947 forced the British to hand over the Gilgit agency back to the Maharaja as per the Indian Independence Act passed by the British Parliament.

On the lapse of "paramountcy" in 1947, British Indian Government handed over the administrative control of all areas of the Gilgit Agency including Hunza to the Kashmir State Government. Accordingly, Brigadier Ghansara Singh was appointed by the Maharaja as the Governor of these areas on 19 July 1947. He arrived in Gilgit on 30 July 1947 along with General Scott, the Chief of Staff of Kashmir State Forces. During their meeting with Major Brown, the Commandant of Gilgit Scouts, Subedar Major Babar Khan and the other Junior Commissioned Officers (JCOs) he was assured that they would serve the State if their demands regarding their service conditions were accepted.

However, when Ghansara Singh took over the administration from Lt. Col. Beacon, the Political Agent on 1 August 1947, the entire office work of the administration came to a grinding halt as all the British officers opted for Pakistan and no replacements from the State had been positioned there. The civil establishment in Gilgit had refused to serve till they were guaranteed higher rates of pay. It appears that both Gilgit Scouts and local as well as non-local civil employees had taken an attitude of noncooperation with the Governor at the instigation of some British officers. To compound matters, all the controlled stores had been spent or distributed and not even an ounce of sugar or a yard of cloth was left in the stores. General Scott returned to Srinagar on 2 August 1947 with a promise to get some assistance.

For next three months, the Governor was a lame duck, he sent letters and telegrams to the Prime Minister and Foreign Secretary at Srinagar informing them about the state of affairs in Gilgit and surrounding areas. However, palace intrigues at Srinagar ensured that these correspondences rarely fetched a reply and accordingly no tangible help came from Srinagar to cement Maharaja's administration in Gilgit. Even General Scott's attempts to highlight the situation in Gilgit fell on deaf ears. It seems as if the Maharaja's administration was too preoccupied by internal intrigues and the problems in Punch and the valley to spare thoughts and resources for a far-flung region. Militarily, no attempts were made to significantly consolidate the Maharaja's hold in Gilgit agency. One company of 5th Kashmir Light Infantry commanded by Captain Durga Singh and located at Bunji, 34 miles short of Gilgit, was replaced by 6 Kashmir Light Infantry comprising of two companies of Sikh and Muslim troops and led by Lt. Col. Abdul Majeed Khan. Services of some British Officers had been retained by the State and consequently 500, strong Gilgit Scouts were being commanded by Major Brown, who was being assisted by Capt. Matheson, Captain Mohammad Sayeed and Lt. Haider of Kashmir Army. During this period, Muslim officers of the State had established contact with the officers of Gilgit Scout with the purpose of establishing Pakistan in Gilgit.

After Pakistan invaded Jammu and Kashmir and Maharaja fled Srinagar for Jammu and acceded to India, there was pandemonium in Gilgit. Rumours were floating that Srinagar had fallen and conspiracies were being hatched by the Gilgit Scouts and elements of State forces. Non-Muslim population was alarmed and approached the Governor who advised them to remain in Gilgit and face whatever was in store for them. In the early hours of November 1, 1947, just after midnight, the house of the Governor was surrounded by about 100 scouts and asked to surrender. The governor surrendered ostensibly with a view to protect the lives of non-Muslim residents. The governor's surrender, however, led to the disintegration of State Forces, with troops killing each other. All the Sikh troops were either killed or ran away to the mountains to save their lives. After the Governor's arrest, a provisional government of "People's Republic of Gilgit and Baltistan" was set up. It was headed by one local Rais Khan and included Major Brown, Captain Ihsan Ali, Capt. Hassan (both of State Forces), Captain Sayeed, Lieutenant Haider, Subedar Major Babar Khan (all three from Gilgit Scouts) and Wazir Wiiayat Ali. On 4 November 1947, Pakistani flag was hoisted at the Gilgit Scouts lines by Major Brown who described his action as a 'coup d' etat and informed Peshawar about the accession of Gilgit to Pakistan. Sir George Cunningham, the new governor of the NWFP, on hearing of Brown's coup in Gilgit instructed him to restore order. Subsequently, the rulers of the enclaves of Hunza and Nagar, within the Gilgit Agency, which were vassals of the Maharaja of Kashmir, also declared their accession to Pakistan.

After capturing Dardistan, the invasion of Baltistan started, which was led by Captain Ihsan Ali and included troops from 6th Kashmir Light Infantry, Gilgit Scouts and about 1,200 combatants from Chitral. The state forces led by Colonel Sher Jung Thapa defended Skardu gallantly for over six months, despite being totally cut-off from rest of the Indian forces. However, the rebels supported by Pakistani forces captured Zojila Pass in May 1948 and infiltrated through Drass, Kargil and other points to threaten Leh. Indian Army had to subsequently use tanks to clear them from Zojila and defend Leh. It is indeed sad that despite heroic resistance having been put up by Thapa and his troops the Indian armed forces could not relieve Skardu and assist the garrison there. The Army's efforts to link up with the garrison were foiled by infiltrators who ambushed the two platoons of Gorkha troops that had been sent to relieve the garrison at Skardu; the Air Force for some inexplicable reasons was reluctant to undertake supply missions to Skardu by *Dakotas*, although they undertook far more risky operations during the war. The air force did airdrop some supplies but they fell far short of the minimum needs of the besieged garrison and the non-Muslim population that had taken refuge in the cantonment. As a result, on 14 August 1948, Skardu garrison led by Thapa surrendered and the control over Baltistan and surrounding areas passed on to Pakistan.

Major Brown had sent frantic wireless messages to Pakistani authorities in Peshawar to take over the area and Pakistan sent Sardar Mohammad Alam as its first political agent. The accession was formalized by signing an agreement with presidents of "Azad Kashmir" and Muslim Conference on 28 April 1949. The agreement legitimized Pakistani administrative control over Northern areas. After the ceasefire, people were put under the control of a Resident who exercised total judicial and administrative control over the area.

Liaqat Ali Khan decided that Gilgit and Baltistan should not be incorporated into Pakistan's democratic structures. As a result the area was kept constitutionally separate from rest of Pakistan and ruled directly by the Ministry of Kashmir Affairs in Karachi. In 1952, the Joint Secretary in the Ministry was made the ex-officio Resident of Northern Areas. In 1967, a separate post of Resident based at Gilgit was created. Though the 1949 agreement lapsed after the promulgation of 1970 Act by President Yahya Khan, Pakistan has refused to return the areas to "Azad Kashmir" despite being told by the courts to do so. Frontier Crimes Regulations (FCR), which treated tribesmen as barbaric and uncivilized and levied collective fines and punishments and had been imposed by the British on the recalcitrant tribes of the Frontier Region, were retained in Northern Areas. In 1963, Pakistan gave away 2,500 square miles of the territory of the former state of Hunza to China as part of Sino-Pak Agreement, despite opposition by Mir of Hunza.

The region has never been represented in Pakistani parliament or even in "Azad Kashmir Assembly." In 1973, Zulfikar Ali Bhutto's government initiated reforms in the Gilgit Baltistan region after abolishing the traditional Miri and Rajgi system and the FCR. In 1970, an Advisory Council with 14 elected members was set up and was converted into Northern Areas Council in 1975, but it continued without any legislative or executive powers and was presided over by the Administrator. In 1999, it was expanded and renamed as Northern Areas Legislative Council (NALC). In 2000, the post of Speaker and in 2002 the post of Deputy Speaker were created. During the tenure of first NALC from 1999 to 2004, it failed to legislate on any subject. It did pass 18 resolutions recommending issues of public interest to Ministry of Kashmir Affairs and Northern Areas (KANA), however, none of these were executed.

The attempts by Zia-ul-Haq to introduce Sunni-Deobandi Islam in the region exacerbated the sense of alienation in Northern Areas. As a result the Sunni Deobandi militant groups, especially Sipah-e-Sahaba, spread their tentacles in this remote tribal region and the Shias and the Ismailis were made to submit to their puritanical aggression. The local population perceived the local administration to be siding with these Sunni extremists. This resulted in the first major violent manifestation of their discontent by the majority Shias in Gilgit in May 1988. Zia put a Special Service Group (SSG) group commanded by then Brigadier Pervez Musharraf to suppress the revolt and Musharraf responded by transporting a large number of Wahabi Pakhtoon tribesmen from the NWFP and Afghanistan to Gilgit to teach the Shias a lesson. These tribesmen massacred hundreds of Shias.

Musharraf also initiated a policy of bringing in Punjabis and Pakhtoons from outside and settling them in Gilgit and Baltistan in order to reduce the Kashmiri Shias to a minority in their traditional land and the process continues to this date. The rapid settling of Punjabis and Pakhtoons from outside has created a sense of acute insecurity among the local Shias. It is widely believed in Pakistan that a Shia airman from Gilgit, wanting to take revenge for the May 1988 carnage, was responsible for the air crash that killed General Zia. After 1988, sectarian riots became a regular feature of Northern Areas. The pattern showed that whenever the populace in Northern Areas demanded their constitutional rights, there were riots. On Zia's death anniversary on 17 August 1993, there were massive riots and over 20 persons were killed before the situation was brought under control by the Army. Army had accused that Shias had amassed weapons in mosques, which included M-46 bombs, brought from Iran. This followed persecution of Shias and a large number of Shias were arrested.

Since 1988, the latent sectarianism coupled with lack of representation has aggravated the sense of alienation in the populace of Northern Areas and have led to the creation of ultra-nationalist political groupings like Balwaristan National Front. During 2003-04, Shias objected to certain portions of the school course curriculum, particularly the contents of Islamiyat and Urdu textbooks and the popular discontentment was so high that the authorities were forced to accept the Shia viewpoint after the violent riots in June 2004. Imam Aga Syed Ziauddin Rizvi, the local Shia cleric, helped the authorities in trying to resolve the issue to the satisfaction of Shias. However, the issue was so emotive that all schools in Northern Areas remained closed for one full year till April 2005 and could only be reopened after controversial portions were removed to the satisfaction of all sects.

The Northern Areas constitute the most backward areas in the entire South Asia and the region seems to have missed the development bus completely. The literacy rates in the region are at 14 per cent far below Pakistan's national average of 31 per cent and the literacy rate of women is abysmally low at 3.5 per cent. There is one doctor for every 6,000 people and one hospital bed for 1,500 people. Less than 10 per cent of the hydroelectric potential of the region has been tapped for local use. This especially is ironic as Pakistan intends to build mega dams at Skardu and Bhasha which will inundate millions of acres of populated fertile lands to provide cheap electricity to rest of Pakistan. Unfortunately, Bhasha Dam has been so planned that the royalty from the Dam will go to NWFP as Article 161(2) of the Pakistani Constitution stipulates that the royalty and the bulk of the net profits earned from a hydroelectric station shall go to the province where the station is situated. The Bhasha Village, which will house only one per cent of the dam, is shown to be in the NWFP; hence earnings from the dam will likely go to the NWFP even though the dam would inundate 32 villages of Diamer District of Northern Areas, with a combined population of 26,000, and thousands of kanals of agricultural land.

The Northern Area has no university and no professional colleges. It has only 12 high schools and two regional colleges with no post graduate facilities. Lack of education has practically closed all avenues of government jobs, thus negating their changes for upliftment. This has led to the demand for reservation as in Indian educational institutions! There are no daily newspapers and no radio or TV stations. The local people drew their subsistence from tourism, which has also declined considerably, and by joining the Northern Light Infantry, recruitment in which has also been reduced considerably.

Of late, people in the region especially in Baltistan have started attempts to reestablish links with all things Tibetan or Ladakhi, in a last-ditch attempt to save their culture from total Iran-style Islamization. They feel culture is more than a question of being Islamic and non-Islamic. They feel threatened from Pakistan's dominant Punjabi culture. According to Syed Abbas Kazml, who is in the forefront of this revival movement, "We have lost our link with the past. To wear our traditional woollen clothes or even to speak Balti is considered a sign of backwardness. We dress like and eat like the Punjabis even though many of their customs are just as foreign to us as those from the West." He has made attempts to protect the pre-Islamic Buddhist architecture of the region. As part of this campaign to defend their culture, the people have started attempts to bring back Tibetan script as they feel that Arabic script is grossly inadequate to bring out the richness in their language. As part of this revival process Baltistan Students Federation has made the *yung drung* (swastika), the ancient Bon symbol of prosperity, as their logo.

Local scholars have taught themselves how to read the Tibetan script and have initiated a dialogue with their counterparts in Ladakh through internet. They research and publish mostly in Urdu, on topics ranging from the ancient Bon tradition to the Gesar epic. Though the Tibetan Buddhism and Bon were replaced over the course of centuries, the process of Islamization has accelerated after the region came under Pakistani control especially after the Iranian revolution but the information age and current soul searching may help Baltistan embrace its ancient diversity. People have accordingly been demanding the opening of Kargil-Skardu bus service to revive their cultural links with Ladakh region especially Kargil and surrounding region. Ladakh and Baltistan share a common history, culture and natural heritage. In fact, prior to 1947, Baltistan was part of the Ladakh Wazarat. They feel that by not allowing the bus service Pakistan is probably preventing their attempts at cultural consolidation and development of cultural linkages across the line of control.

"Rebellion and resentment, that have been brewing among people of the Northern Areas, is fast reaching a crescendo against persecution by the Pakistani armed forces, the continuing denial of legal and political rights, and devious attempts at demographic engineering in this strategic region." The acts of violence In Gilgit area are indicative of the damage being done to Northern Areas in the absence of any genuine democratic and constitutional mechanism to solve their problems. The people feel that they are non-citizens or at best second-class citizens. The Kargil episode, which involved a large number of casualties of *jawans* from the area, added a whole new set of grievances. As in many other areas of Pakistan, the federal government's hand is seen behind sectarian terrorism, which is believed to be a tool being used to divide the people. This deep mistrust of government is the main reason behind attacks on state property and officials, whenever any sectarian incident takes place or any other serious complaint emerges. It is also an indicator of the peoples' lack of ownership of government properties and facilities.

The region is legally the part of India and the Indian Government has of late started voicing its concern on the denial of constitutional rights to the people of the region. The alienation of the population in this crucial region provides India a good leverage against Pakistan and diminishes the importance of valley-based groups. The demand by the people of Baltistan to open a bus-link between Kargil and Skardu must be encouraged as it will reunite families divided for 58 years, and expose the people of this deprived region to the constitutional rights and autonomy being enjoyed by the people of Kargil and Ladakh.

Besides Pakistan held Kashmir territory being a breeding ground for anti-India terrorists, recently Bangladesh has also emerged as another pincer against India in terrorism. In fact, the Hizbullah Jamaat-e-Islami (HUJI) has a large network with Bangladesh and connected with the Al-Qaeda operations in Indonesia through the Jamaat-e-Islamiyah. Bangladesh trained terrorists have carried out murderous attacks against Indians in Mumbai, Bangalore and Hyderabad utilizing the millions of illegal immigrants from Bangladesh in India. We need to impose some costs on Bangladesh for this gross betrayal since without Indian Army, Bangladesh could never have come into existence so costlessly for them.

We could for example now demand territory from Bangladesh for all those illegal Bangladeshis settled in India. After all, Partition was for those Muslims who could not bear to live with Hindus. Hence, the territory of Bangladesh should be reduced in proportion to millions of Bangladesis that have come to India, and the Hindus that have been pushed out since 1947. Strategically, northern one-third of Bangladesh from the horizontal line Sylhet to Khulna northwards could be annexed if Bangladesh goes to war with us.

Otherwise, what is the alternative? Walk meekly to death expecting that our "sober" responses will be rewarded by our neighbours and their patrons? We will be back to 1100 AD, fooled into suicidal credulity. We should not be ghouls for punishment anymore from terrorists and their patrons. This is *Kaliyug*, and hence there is no room for *sattvic* responses to evil people. Hindu religion has a concept of *apat dharma* propounded by Bhishmacharya in *Mahabharata* to Arjuna and we should invoke it in our fight against terrorism.

While Pakistan-abetted Islamic fundamentalists are the sheet anchor of the terrorist menace in Kashmir, there is a recent trend for these terrorists to penetrate the vast mainland of the Indian peninsula to seek local recruits as well as to strike terror nation-wide. The Students of Islamic Movement of India (SIMI), now banned as a terrorist organization, is one such recruiting agency.

Terrorists' attacks are not targeted mainly at security forces and government establishments in Kashmir, but have expanded to include strikes against India's economic and strategic assets, nation-wide. Thus Indian railway networks, Mumbai stock market, the atomic energy establishment and the Indian Institute of Science have come within the purview of terrorists' goals.

The metropolis in India has thus become a terror target in keeping with the trend noticeable around the world. From New York to Madrid to London and Mumbai, urban terror has become a major trend—bigger the city, greater the fallout.

A new pattern of attacks on commuter and mass transport system has also emerged. In March 2004, Madrid's train network was hit by a series of explosions at the rush hour. In all 191 people were killed and over 1,700 wounded. In July 2005, a series of coordinated bomb-blasts, now known as 7/11, struck London's underground rail during the morning rush hour, killing 88 people.

Terror attacks on big cities make the maximum public and media impact with its identifiable landmarks, its heterogenous mix of citizens. City-based media and 24x7 news channels ensure immediate coverage. For patrons of terrorists, the resultant mayhem and carnage needs to be watched and the chaos and panic is a measure of the "success" of their acts. The Mumbai serial blasts on 11 July 2006 followed this pattern timing it for the "rush-hour" in the evening.

India has now witnessed a series of terrorist attacks on its major cities, since the Mumbai serials blasts. In Delhi, some of the earlier major attacks were the 22 May 2005 blast in two cinema-halls, the 29 October 2005 serial blasts and the Deepavali eve blasts in Sarojini Nagar in 2005. Subsequently, there was an attack on the Indian Institute of Science (IISc), Bangalore. Since 2005, 273 people have been killed, including five terrorists and 268 civilians, and many more injured and properties wrecked in such attacks on the Indian metropolises.[10]

The Mumbai Police Commissioner identified the ISI as being the mastermind of the Mumbai terror attacks with the help of Pakistan-based terrorist outfits LeT and Jaish-e-Mohammed (JeM) associating local SIMI members, especially the 26/11 terrorist take over of Mumbai's Taj Hotel and other places. The idea of dressing the Pak terrorists in Hindu atire and 'tikka' on their foreheads was to enable some Indians to propagate that it was an act of 'Hindu Terror'. But the chance capture alive of Kasab explode the fake narrative after kasad confessed to being from Pakistan. Nearly 21 people were arrested from different parts of the country within days

[10]See T. K. Singh, "Terror Trends," *Strategic Analysis*, IDSA, New Delhi, September 2006.

in connection with the incident. One of them, arrested from J&K on 23 August 2006, during questioning claimed that 17 members of the Pakistan- based Lashkar-e-Taiba (LeT) were involved in carrying out the attacks, of which 16 have returned back safely and one went missing. The missing terrorist, Salim, was finally identified among the dead in the train bomb blast at Mahim. The police investiga-tions have also identified the Students Islamic Movement of India (SIMI) as being involved with the LeT in executing the attacks. SIMI has a strong network across India and in recent years has become a principal ally of nearly all major Islamist terrorist groups.

Since 1997, Delhi has witnessed 26 major bomb blasts killing in all 92 people and injuring more than 600. Among the incidents, the 10/29 (2005) blasts was the most serious—killing 62 persons and injuring 155. The explosion occurred almost simultaneously at two busy market places in Delhi and one in a Delhi Transport Cooperation bus. The first high-intensity incident was on 13 December 2001, viz. the attack on Parliament in which 11 were killed and 30 injured. Investigators later found the attack was jointly executed by the Pakistan-based LeT and JeM.

The terrorist attack in the IISc campus in Bangalore on 28 December 2005 represents a departure from targeting security forces personnel and ordinary civilians. In this case, scientists and scholars were the targets. The attack took place in the middle of an International Conference organized by the Operational Research Society of India. A former professor was killed and five persons were injured when an unidentified gunman opened fire and lobbed grenades in the IISc campus. The attack, as later revealed, was carried out by a LeT member, who was also the outfit's south Indian commander, Abdul Rehman. He was subsequently arrested. The terrorist motive in this case was to target the Indian IT industry and instill fear in the scientific community and research institutes.

On 6 March 2005, a Delhi-based LeT cell was eliminated, that hatched a plot to attack a series of IT centres of India in connivance with the banned SIMI. All these indicated an expanding terrorist network in the southern part of the country and the targeting of the symbols of emerging India—the IT sector, scientific establishments and nuclear power plants. The arrested terrorists were also planning to attack the Indian Military Academy (IMA) in Dehradun.

The then National Security Advisor, M. K. Narayanan, stated on 28 July 2006 that there was a serious threat from the LeT to nuclear installations in the country. Writing in *Strategic Studies* (2002), an in-house journal of Pakistan's Institute of Strategic Studies in Islamabad, a hard-line analyst, Dr. Shireen Mazari, has opined: "Of all South Asian states, India's nuclear facilities are perhaps the most vulnerable to nuclear terrorism ... aggravated by its thriving underworld and over a dozen insurgencies.. ." Sri Lanka Government has also warned that the micro-light aircrafts of the erstwhile LTTE could threaten India's nuclear installations in Kalpakkam near Chennai.

While Islamic fundamentalist-led terrorism is the main sheet-anchor for undermining India's national security, there are also several other insurgencies around the country getting converted to terrorist threats—the Naxalites, ULFA, PWG, Nagas, TNLU, Manipuris, etc. Statistics since January 2004-March 2007 show that of the 4,000 odd persons killed in terrorist violence in India, show that 41 per cent died due to Islamic terrorists, 27 per cent due to left-wing extremists such as Maoists and Naxalites in 14 states of the nation, and 20 per cent due to fatalities from insurgencies in the Northeast. There is some evidence of coordination and networking of these terrorist outfits with Al-Qaeda and LTTE. This means that India now faces a Terror Incorporated International, and hence terrorists activities in other nations affect such as Nepal, Afghanistan and Sri Lanka, even Iraq, India's national security and long-term national interests.

There is an another perfidious angle to Islamic terrorism confronting India. The large Muslim population of India is being sandwiched between the accusation that they are not cooperating with the law and order forces in exposing the sleeper terrorist cells living in their "Mohallas" (neighbourhood), and the ire of the terrorists against India's Muslims for not enthusiastically contributing to the terror goal of establishing a Darul Islam in India by violence and securing capitulation. Hence, the terrorist are now targeting Islamic centres or population as in the bombing of the Malegoan's *Masjid*, Hyderabad's Mecca *Masjid*, Delhi Jama *Masjid* and the Samjautha Express train. External Islamic terrorists are targeting Indian Muslims in order for them to become cannon-fodder in the destabilization of Indian civil society. Such targeted attacks to radicalize Muslims is also part of terror strategy. On 26 August, 2007 Hyderabad again intnessed in horror 34 dead, some of them Muslims in two bomb explosions in a drama venue and a restaurant.

The nation has had enough make-up calls. We can wake up those in authority who are sleeping, but not those who are feigning sleep in the name of secularism.

CHAPTER IV

Global Terror Infrastructure and Implications for India

Global terrorism is recognized today as one of the gravest threats confronting humanity. What has made terrorism more lethal and widespread is the availability of modern technology and global communication networks, especially satellite phones and the internet and the adoption of "suicide" tactics. The effectiveness of terrorism is magnified mass media and multiplied by the panic reactions of targeted societies by the visualization on living room TVs. Terrorist tactics, thus, derive comparative advantage as a technique, viz. the rapid spread of images, its immediate impact, and enabling communities that lie at the extreme edge of frustration to make them feel that their presence is felt.

Undeniably, religious faith-based terrorism *especially Islamic Fundamentalist sustained terror,* which is backed by strong external linkages and connectivity, is the defining global threat today. Intricate networking connects vast numbers of radical Islamist terrorist groups, nurtured on the rabid Islamic preaching of paradise after death is responsible for the insane suicide missions of able bodied persons.

World-wide operations of terrorist groups reveal that an entirely new breed of terrorists has emerged. Terrorist outfits today have a transnational reach. New support structures and modern global financing mechanisms are being created. Cipher coding of messages is becoming more sophisticated.

There are three major areas on which to concentrate in formulating a counter-terrorist strategy in the fight against international terrorism

First, penetration of the hardcore of terrorist planning where actual operations are conceived and implemented; and *second*, the techniques and propaganda by which sympathy is generated for the objectives of particular cells, where recruits are inspired to sign-up and where hiding places are created. *Third*, the structure of the policy by which terrorists can be disadvantaged and set-back in planning terrorist operations. For example, penetration of informers deep into the planning cells of terrorist organization and creating disinformation, or, reducing the flow of funds and money supply to terrorist capability to acquire weapons, recruit cadres, establish training facilities and state-or-the-art secure communications. Although not all terrorist acts require large funds, the need for funds is determined by the size and area of the operation, the focus here would be on the method of transfer of funds, locating and eliminating hawala operators etc. The nation has now has been forewarned by the US State Department in its 2006 *Country Terrorism Reports* (published on 30 April 2007) in which it is stated that terrorist organizations such as Jaish-e-Mohammed have used Indian banks, commodities markets, and stock exchanges not only to fund terror but earn high dividends and interest on their ill-gotten funds!

The *modus operandi* employed by terrorist outfits to generate funds has been brought out by India's National Security Adviser, M. K. Narayanan, at the 43rd Munich Conference on Security Policy held on 11 February 2007:

(i) *Voluntary contributions:* from individuals, members of expatriate communities, and organizations that sympathize with the broad objectives of the terrorist organization. The erstwhile LTTE in

Sri Lanka and the Al Qaeda, regularly received sizeable contributions through such means.

(ii) *Forced/Compulsory donations:* Ethnic, ideological and religious terrorists are known to use the technique of forced or compulsory donations on special occasions such as religious festivals, sending round of "collection boxes" is fairly common, and provides anonymity as well. Compulsory subscriptions to pro-terrorist publications have laterally become an important avenue for generation of funds. The Pakistan-based Lashkar-e-Toeba's monthly, *Majalah-al-Dawana*, and its weekly magazine, *Al Ghazwa*, are two prime examples.

(iii) *State support/sponsorship:* The Lashkar-e-Toeba, the Hizbul Mujahideen and the Al Badr (which operate in India) are well patronized, including through provision of funds, by certain official agencies across the border. Shared objectives such as involvement in "Low-Intensity Conflict" provide the excuse for such official support. A tentative estimate of funds made available to such terrorist outfits annually is in the region of a few million dollars.

(iv) *Extortion and use of coercive methods:* Many terrorist outfits today imitate criminal enterprises. Intimidation of small businesses, individuals and even some State enterprises to extort funds has become common. Association with Criminal Syndicates—*Jehadi* and non-*jehadi* terrorist outfits seek, and enter into, partnerships with Organized Criminal Syndicates, and outsource fund-raising to the latter. This is largely true of metropolitan cities. It takes many forms, but mainly bank robberies and kidnapping for ransom.

(v) *Utilisation of legitimate business enterprises:* Terrorist outfits set up legitimate business enterprises, viz. restaurants, real estate, shipping, etc. and utilize part of the proceeds to siphon off funds for terrorist activities. Among terrorist outfits, the LTTE had a very well-established network of legitimate businesses, worth about

$2 billion, which provide both funds as well as logistics for their activities. Jehadi terrorist organizations have begun to follow the example of the LTTE.

(vi) *Stock market operations:* Isolated instances of terrorist outfits manipulating the stock markets to raise funds for their operations have been reported. Stock Exchanges in Mumbai and Chennai (India) have, on occasions, reported that fictitious or notional companies were engaging in stock-market operations. Some of these companies were later traced to terrorist outfits. Misuse of banking channels—legitimate banking channels are regularly being used to fund terrorist operations. Many instances of funds received *via* banking channels from so-called safe locations such as Dubai and UAE intended for terrorist organizations have been detected by Indian Counter-Terrorist Agencies. Each individual transaction tends to be small so as not to attract attention and to avoid detection. Use of both real, and fraudulent, ATM cards has also been resorted to at times. The UPA government's introduction of Participatory Notes (PN) instrument which has been exempted for some mysterious reason from disclosing the owners and sources of funds in the purchase and sales of the PNs., has been continued for some inexplicable reason during the last seven years by the Modi Government. The opportunity that the Modi Government to carry out a Israeli type of bombardment of Pakistan's camps for training of Islamic fanatic terrorist was such easier then than now since the Chinese and their junior partner have now openly and overtly begun packing Pakistan. The Ministry of Finance has placed the PNs outside the serious surveillance of the SEBI, making it an ideal financial instrument of the terrorists. The PNs now account for 53 per cent of the foreign financial flows into India.

(vii) *Narcotics:* Funds from drug cultivation and trafficking in narcotics are extensively used to fund terrorist outfits. Both jehadi outfits and the LTTE rely heavily on such funds for their activities.

The sharp rise in opium cultivation in Afghanistan—which has more than doubled during the past few years—raises concerns of more funds becoming available to terrorists. According to Indian Agencies, at least 1/8th of their major interdictions reveal a drugs-terrorist nexus.

(viii) _*Counterfeit currency:* Counterfeiting of currency is currently a favourite method being adopted (by Agencies across the border) to fund terrorist activities directed at India. Large amounts of high quality counterfeit Indian currency are detected each year—the normal route being *via* Nepal and Bangladesh.

(ix) *Charities:* An important source of funds to jehadi terrorist outfits are religious charities. This has been widely exposed in the August 2007 Hyderabad bombings. Sincere believers contributing to charities are perhaps unaware that a sizeable portion of the funds go to fund terrorist activities and terrorist outfits. Many of the charities are already designated as "Terrorist Front Organizations"; yet most continue to operate under new labels. The Al Rashid Trust went through several changes in nomenclature, while the banned International Islamic Relief morphed into the Sanabil Al Khir Foundation. Conduits through which such funds find their way to terrorist organizations include established banking channels such as the Habib Bank in Pakistan.

These nine sources of funding of terrorist activities in India have also been reiterated in the US State Department's 2007 *Country Review on Terrorism*. Moving funds for terrorist purposes to the actual locale where a terrorist act is perpetrated is a carefully executed exercise. Terrorist outfits, as a rule, employ money laundering techniques so as to evade detection by Enforcement Agencies. The most popular means employed in South Asia for laundering funds is the "underground and parallel banking system" which ensures placing of funds without actual or visible movement of money. This is popularly called as "hawala."

A combination of conventional money laundering techniques, with placement of funds utilizing the "underground and parallel banking system" has made it extremely difficult to track funds utilized for terrorist purposes, since no audit or paper trail is available. The globalization of terror, and the ability of terrorists to exploit state-of-the-art technology, further enhances their capability to move "hot money" across international borders. It has also facilitated "narco-terrorism" very greatly.

Narco-terrorism refers to the nexus between narcotics and terrorism. Since the sources of terrorism in India lie beyond the domestic frontiers in Pakistan and elsewhere, the growth of illicit narcotics trade funds terrorist activities in India. Afghanistan and the NWEP of Pakistan are the biggest producers of opium in the world, which generates huge sums of money in the international market. The drug proceeds are used by the Pakistan government and the non-government agencies to destabilize India. The LTTE was the most efficient drug-runner, and co-ordinates the smuggling from its office in Palermo Sicily in Italy.

Sponsoring terrorism is an expensive affair and money for killing, kidnapping and sabotage does not come through proper channels. It comes through illegal and unofficial channels. It fetches cash in sackfuls for one kilogram of heroin from the Golden Crescent that costs approximately one lakh rupees in South Asia, fetches nearly a crore of rupees in the US market. The figure varies from place to place, which further depends on the law and order situation. The price for heroin originating from the Golden Crescent ranges from Rs. 30 lakhs to Rs. 1 crore a kg. *It is worth noting that Pakistani heroin and Colombian marijuana are the most demanded narcotic drugs in the US and the European countries.* The volume of money these drugs generate in the West is mind boggling. It is because of the enormous money involved in the illicit drug trade that terrorists have established links with drug traffickers, smugglers and underworld dons to meet the expenses for "operation terrorism."

The hypothesis that drug trafficking funds terrorist activities is based on certain facts:

1. The economy of narcotics-producing countries is dependent on the illegal drugs trade. Unless they have an alternative economy, the illicit narcotic drugs trade would continue irrespective of strict legislation.
2. *Afghanistan is the biggest illicit opium producing* (4,600 per annum, 1999 of the world's total 6,000 metric tons) country in the world. Poppy cultivation is done in 18 out of the total 31 provinces of Afghanistan. If Taliban take over the central government as per US decision and the vaccum is not filled by India by boots on the ground of the Indian armed forces, then Taliban Pakistan terror will force multiply the terrorists to attack India. Event of June 27, 2021 in Jammu is a dress rehearsal of what is to come. Disremembering Jammu, Kashmir and Ladakh from the Indian mailand can be achieved by a Pakistan-China axis. If that happens due to the procrastination of Modi Government, Balkanisation of India is next.
3. Narcotic drugs are the most lucrative commodity that generate quick money without paper work. The business transaction is done in hard cash and no document is left as evidence for legal action.
4. The drug proceeds are laundered through numerous legal and illegal financial institutions and petty business enterprises.
5. Terrorism needs huge sums of money to carry out its operation. Since it is difficult to acquire that sum from official and legal sources, terrorists approach drug syndicates and underworld dons for cooperation.

6. The criminal dons and drug smugglers too find the proposal attractive because it gives them an opportunity to collaborate with aspirants of political power (terrorists) and thereby gives them access to politics in due course of time. The criminalization of politics is the result of the same nexus.
7. The Pakistani Drug Syndicate runs a parallel economy in connivance with political and military establishments to destabilize India. *According to the UN Report, Pakistan's heroin industry in terms of turnover is estimated at approximately Rs. 154 billion, i.e. 6 per cent of it's GDP of 2002-03, which is 20-25 per cent of the total estimated shadow economy.* It also reported that Pakistan earned US $3.5 billion from export of heroin in 2002.

General Zia's involvement in drug trafficking came to light only after his death when the Minister of State for Narcotics, Mian Muzaffar Shah, revealed that Pakistani drug syndicates grew under the patronage of General Zia. *Raza Qureshi, a Pakistan drug trafficker, who was arrested by the Norwegian Police at Oslo's Fornebu Airport in 1984, exposed* Zia's drug connection. *The Norwegian Police disclosed three names of Pakistani nationals—Tahir Butt, Munawar Hussain and Hamid Hussam* patronized by General Zia. The Norwegian Police visited Islamabad to investigate the matter and indicted these three for drug crimes. But the Pakistan Government did not arrest them because of their political connections. Finally, when the Norwegian Government complained against inaction by the law enforcement agencies and threatened diplomatic action, these three were arrested.

One of the culprits, Hamid Hussain, was not only the vice-president of *Government-owned Habib Bank, but was as close as a son to the wife of General Zia ul Haq*. According to one reliable report, he had handled Zia's account, and had used banking channels to launder drug proceeds. The most chilling revelation confirming Zia's drug connection was the case of one of his ADCs, whose name was not disclosed. The ADC concealed heroin in 100 precious lamps to be gifted by General Zia to the delegates at a special session of the UN General Assembly. General Zia suddenly changed his programme to travel *via* Iran and Iraq. In the process of shifting his baggage, one of the lamps broke spreading heroin at New York Airport. Apparently, the customs official checked all the lamps which were filled with heroin and seized them. What action followed no one seems to know even today.

The situation, however, did not change when Benazir Bhutto in late 1980s came to power. She exposed General Zia because it suited her political agenda, but her husband Zardari is well known for his criminal connections and her government was dismissed on corruption charges. In so far as Benazir's Peoples Party (PPP) is concerned, during personal interaction of Indian investigating officials with Pakistani prisoners under NDPS Act languishing in Jammu Central Jail, they were told that the PPP members were directly involved in the drugs trade. The prisoner himself was a cousin of PPP's Lahore President. Lahore is one of the centres for narcotic drugs trade in Pakistan.

Another equally important drug dealer, Malik Waris Khan Afridi, was appointed by Benazir as Minister of state for Tribal Affairs. He was elected on a PPP ticket from Khyber Agency (N-33, Tribal Areas VII) in 1988. His commitment to PPP was so strong that he tried to save her government by bribing members against the no-confidence motion tabled by Nawaz Sharif in 1989. After the fall of the Benazir Government he was convicted for smuggling of opium and hashish from Khyber Agency. Ms Bhutto's money launderer, Ms Farida Atairllah, is also connected to a very important Indian political family, and has stayed in their official accommodation. She was also the guest of honour in a very private but celebrated wedding in the family.

Nor was Benazir's rival untainted by such charges. Hazi Iqbal Beg, a Pakistani drug dealer, was a Lahore-based landlord and owner of innumerable businesses. Beg along with his partners, Sohail Butt (brother-in-law of Nawaz Sharif) and Shaukat Ali Bhatti, were elected members of the Punjab Legislative Assembly on the ticket of Islamic Jahmuri Ittehad (IJI), a political party formed by an ISI Chief General Hamid Gul. Nawaz Sharif maintained close association with Beg and helped him acquire denationalized industrial units including the Muslim Commercial Bank where he (Sharif) is a *benami* partner.

Beg continued to nurture his ties with the Pakistani premier and simultaneously funded election of Mehraj Khalid of PPP who later became Chief Minister of Punjab. Beg thus remained loyal to both Sharif and Benazir. After the fall of Benazir's Government, he was charge-sheeted for narcotic drugs smuggling. However, his close association with Sharif got him released on bail. That was the last one heard of him.

These are some of the many instances of the drug syndicate's control over Pakistan politics. There are hundreds of political leaders into drug business in Pakistan. The very fact that South West Asia (Pak-Afghan) is the biggest supplier of heroin the international market and that Pakistan earns billion of dollars from export of refined heroin, substantiates that the narcotic drugs trade goes on under the nose of government law enforcement agencies. Since Pakistani political leaders are beneficiaries of the international drug trade, it is not possible to keep intelligence and army away from the political scene, especially in the light of the fact that these two play a significant role in Pakistan politics.

A noted American scholar, Selig Harrison, has aptly said that Pakistan has ten 'Noriegas' (Noriega was Panama's Drug Lord Head of State, now deposed and in US jail) who are very high up in the military.

Hawala Operations in India

The need to track the sources for funding terrorism was realized way back in 1986 when the UN General Assembly for the first time drafted a *Convention against Recruitment, Use, Finance, and Training of Mercenaries in 1986.* This convention was adopted without a vote on 4 December 1989. In 1994, the General Assembly called attention to the growing connection between drug traffickers and mercenaries. Recalling these resolutions, the *International Convention for the Suppression of the Financing Terrorism was adopted by the UN General Assembly* on 9 December 1999 without a vote.

India has been the victim of state-sponsored terrorism for the last two decades. There is no doubt that the Pakistan Government in collaboration with the ISI uses proceeds of illicit narcotic drugs and small arms trade to fund terrorism in India. Pakistan also aims to create ethnic division in the social fabric of the country by exploiting the religious sentiments and economic backwardness of Muslims in the bordering states of Jammu and Kashmir, Punjab, Rajasthan, Assam, Nagaland, Manipur and other states.

Hawala is a system through which money is transferred from one part of the world to another without following the normal banking channels.

This system has been in existence for a long time in India and other Asian countries. Some *Hawala* operators feel that it is an extension of the 'Hundi' system of money transfer that came into existence during the Mughal rule in India. This was started by the Sindhi community to avoid dacoity and highway robberies during money transfers. Later, sometime around World War II, Muslims going from Kerala to the Persian Gulf adopted the system of giving a coded message sent by post to deliver the money to people in Kerala. Since the Indian rupee was legal tender in the entire region, the transaction did not suffer from cross-currency exchange rates.

With the revolution in communications, messages through post got replaced by telephone and later by fax; and, now by e-mail. In the process, the scope of *Hawala* transactions got enlarged.

According to one account, *Hawala* in Urdu means "reference" and in Arabic means "trust," is in fact an unauthorized underground banking system used by people from different walks of life for a variety of reasons.

The *Hawala* system is known to be exploited by militants all over the world for financing their activities, to purchase arms, to send funds (ISI, Mohhamed Atta, Dawood Ibrahim, Mohammed Ansari, etc. are a few well-known names who have exploited this system for overt or covert funding of terrorist activities), and to finance films.

Narcotics dealers also use the *Hawala* system for siphoning off their illegally earned for financing the terrorist activities and underground deals.

An official US report shows that tax havens harbour deposits around US dollars five trillion and the US Government itself loses about US $70 billion by way of tax. According to one estimate, in 1990, drug traffickers earned a staggering profit of Rs. 20,000 crores in foreign exchange. A part of the proceeds returned to India through the *Hawala* route to influence such businesses.

Pakistan Prime Minister Shaukat Aziz, a former executive vice-president of the World Bank, said $2 billion to $5 billion is moved through the "*Hawala* system annually in Pakistan," more than the amount of foreign transfers through the country's banking system.

Many countries, including India, have already in place a legal framework for tackling the funding of terrorism. Several—India included—have specific legislations to prevent financing of terrorism. India has the (a) Foreign Exchange Management Act, 1999; (b) Narcotic Drugs and Psychotropic Substances Act, 2003; and (c) Prevention of Money Laundering Act, 2003 (which entered into force in July, 2005); apart from provisions in other Acts such as the Unlawful Activities (Prevention) Act of 1967 as amended in 2004, to deal specifically with the threat of terrorism.

Adoption by the UN General Assembly of the UN Global Counter-Terrorism Strategy has enabled a global consensus to emerge on measures that States must undertake to prevent and combat terrorism. India is committed to fully implementing the UN Global Counter-Terrorism Strategy, including measures against the financing of terrorism. India has also joined the International Convention for the Suppression of Financing of Terrorism. We have established the necessary legal, regulatory and administrative framework for combating money laundering and financing of terrorism. A Financial Intelligence Unit-India is already in operation and will be the nodal agency responsible for receiving, processing, analysing and disseminating information relating to suspect financial transactions to intelligence and enforcement agencies.

The importance of international cooperation in combating global terrorism, in all its dimensions, cannot be over-stressed. Only by demonstrating zero tolerance to acts of terrorism committed anywhere in the world, and by working together, including sharing of intelligence on terrorist activities, can we effectively counter the terrorist threat. States must refrain from organizing, instigating, facilitating, participating in, financing, encouraging or tolerating terrorist activities. They must take appropriate measures to ensure that their territories are not used for setting up terrorist infrastructures or training camps ends. India must set an example by giving priority to smashing the terror-financing and clandestine business empire of the LTTE which is anchored in Tamil Nadu, Bangalore and Mumbai. We should no more take a non-chalant attitude to the LTTE, if we want to dent the Terror Incorporated that has emerged within the country.

Facts about the LTTE[11]

The Liberation Tigers of the Tamil Eelam (LTTE) was founded by Vellupillai Prabhakaran on 5 March 1976, the day he conducted a successful bank robbery in Puttur. After a few years of militancy, there was a split thus was created the People's Liberation Organization of Tamil Eelam (PLOTE) by Uma Maheswaran; thereafter many splinter groups emerged. At one time, thirty-seven groups were existing; five were prominent—LTTE, TELO, EPRLF, PLOT and EROS. In due course, LTTE by betrayal and internecine assassinations emerged as the most powerful terrorist organization in Sri Lanka. The ideology of violence of the LTTE is drawn from the Dravidian "National" Movement in Tamil Nadu in the 1950s and 1960s. The cult of martyrdom and the ideology of vengeance are based on appeals to a misinterpreted heroic past. Its leader, V. Prabhakaran, is a character of deep suspicion, fanatic outlook, relentless pursuit of vengeance and utter disregard for human life. Fortunately, the advent of the Rajapaksa brothers in the Sri Lanka Government a decisive drive against the LTTE by the Sri Lanka Government decimated the LTTE by, May 19, 2009, when Supremo of LTTE V. Prabhakaran was shot dead on the beach by Sri Lankan forces. Today, the rump LTTE abroad has been reduced to petitioning the Europeans bleeding hearts for a "Genocide" Commission to indict the Sri Lankan Government.

[11] See Swamy, Subramanian, *Sri Lanka in Crisis: India's Options*, Har-Anand, 2007.

Nevertheless, it is still worth studying the modus operandi of the LTTE.

The LTTE terror strategy had four key components:

(i) the use of times of peace to prepare for war, in line with the Maoist doctrine of "retreat and recuperate";
(ii) an attempt to attain total control over the Tamil struggle to gain legitimacy as the sole representative of Sri Lankan Tamils— it is with this motive that the LTTE has eliminated almost all opposition to it;
(iii) a subordination of the political struggle to the military one—hence, it is not interested in a political solution through dialogue; and,
(iv) a mixture of guerrilla and conventional warfare tactics in battle.

In addition, the Tigers made use of suicide bombers as a tactic. Though many militant groups followed this technique, the LTTE is one of the few organizations to adopt it as an article of faith. A separate unit known as the "Black Tigers" existed to organize attacks on civilian and military targets and eliminate key leaders by these means.

The "paws" of the LTTE extend worldwide from Canada and the United States in the West to Australia in the east, due to the presence of Sri Lankan Tamils in those countries who had fled from the conflict in Sri Lanka. Of late, due to crackdowns on the LTTE, by the United States, Canada, India and South Africa, their support base has narrowed. But their links exist in some West European countries like Britain and Germany, Nordic countries, besides Australia, Thailand, Myanmar, Cambodia, and South Africa. India was once sympathetic towards the LTTE, but soon after dismissal of the DMK State Government in 1991 and the assassination of Rajiv Gandhi, the LTTE has been discredited. Its support is clandestine and has to be purchased.

The funds for the LTTE came from three major sources:

1. *Diaspora contribution*: The major source of funding is by the Sri Lankan Tamil expatriates living in developed countries.
2. *Extortion*: The LTTE also collects money from the people living in areas controlled by it in Sri Lanka as taxation.
3. *Narcotics:* The Tigers are also earning huge amounts of money through the drugs trade, as Sri Lanka is strategically located between the "Golden Crescent" and the "Golden Triangle."

It is this large funding which had enabled the LTTE to increase its firepower by acquiring sophisticated weapons and weapon systems including surface-to-air missiles. The Tigers also received from the Sri Lankan Government, incredible as it may appear, during 1989-92, to assist their fight against the IPKF, weapons captured from the Lankan Army.

The LTTE is one of the few groups in the world, along with the Hizbollah, the Hamas and the Kurdistan Workers Party (PKK) of Turkey, to have an elite suicide squad. Even since the first suicide attack by the Hizbollah in 1983 in Beirut, in which more than 150 American and French Peace-Keepers were killed, there have been more than 250 suicide attacks by various groups all over the world. Of these attacks, the Black Tigers alone had carried out 150; more than those carried out by all other groups put together. They are the only group which succeeded in assassinating two heads of government—Rajiv Gandhi as former Prime Minister and Premadasa as serving President of Sri Lanka.

In his book, Dr. Robert Pape[12] quotes the LTTE as defending suicide bombing as ensuring maximum damage with minimum loss of life.

How is it that the LTTE had succeeded in sustaining its suicide wing? *First,* the entire LTTE cadre were brain-washed to have a

[12] *Dying to Win: The Strategic Logic of Suicide Terrorism*, Random House, 2007.

suicide psychology. This brain-washing was facilitated by recruitment of child soldiers, whose innocent minds were easy targets for brain- washing. Each and every cadre, including the leader Prabhakaran, carry a cyanide capsule necklace, ceremoniously place by local leader in a "passing-out parade" to be bit into, if captured. The Black Tigers are to give up life, deliberately for achieving an organizational target. They are brain-washed to hate their target if it is to be an assassination. For this, the targeted person has not only to be anti-LTTE, but someone who can be portrayed as having betrayed the Tamil cause. Sri Lanka's Foreign Ministe Kadirgama was an easy target because he was a Tamil who was with the Sinhala majority-led government

Second, the glorification of the Black Tigers by the LTTE makes it prestigious. Every year, 5 July was celebrated by the LTTE as the day of the Black Tigers. (It was on 5 July 1987 that the first suicide attack was perpetrated by the LTTE, when it is claimed that LTTE's "Captain" Millar drove a truck full of explosives into a Sri Lankan Army camp, killing nearly forty soldiers.) On this particular day, an eternal lamp is lighted in front of the tombstone of every Black Tiger, who had lost his or her life. The LTTE flag is hoisted and the parents of the Black Tigers, who had sacrificed their lives, are honoured. Dhanu, the "Black Tigress" who took the life of Rajiv Gandhi in 1991 was indirectly honoured by posthumously decorating her late father, an obscure poet who had died in 1979. Since Prabhakaran did not have the nerve to decorate Dhanu, he honoured her father. The LTTE radio also broadcasts the brave deeds of the Black Tigers with their operational details.

Third, the Black Tigers lead most of the suicide military operations of the LTTE, especially its attack on the Sri Lankan Army camps. The Black Tigers, armed with explosives, drive directly into the army camp, catching the Sri Lankan Army totally by surprise and causing maximum damage. Before the Army recovers from its initial shock, the regular cadres of the LTTE attack, making maximum use of the sacrifice by the Black Tigers. The Black Tigers, being the "Leading Force" of any military operation, have a romantic and hero attraction for the cadres.

Fourth, the success rate of the Black Tigers, because of the surprise element of their missions, makes them very popular. In most of the cases, except on a couple of rare occasions, the Black Tigers have succeeded in achieving their mission. Chandrika Kumaratunga was one of the few targets who luckily survived and escaped the Black Tigers assassination attempt. Their ability to penetrate the tough security not only in Colombo, but in other places also and carry out its mission, normally make the Black Tigers appear invincible in their mission. In case of Chandrika, the LTTE rationalized its failure by chanting that she "has to be lucky every time," while the suicide bombers "have to lucky just once." A sick mentality!

Fifth, the Black Tigers have an additional advantage—they can meet the leader of the LTTE, Prabhakaran, considered a demi-god. Since his public appearances are rare for security reasons, meeting Prabhakaran is a lifetime goal for many of the young cadres of the LTTE. Before the suicide mission, the Black Tigers have their "Last Supper" with the leader, which is considered a lifetime honour for its cadres.

Sixth, women cadres dominate Black Tigers. Nearly one-third of the Black Tigers are women. The presence of women in the suicide squad represents an assertion of gender equality that the ostensibly LTTE preaches, and attracts women especially those with grievances about their maltreatment at the hands of men or Sri Lankan soldiers.

Finally, since the LTTE does not have an articulated ideology that could impress and motivate its cadres, the Black Tigers, to a great extent, motivate the cadres by their action and sacrifice, much as a cinema idol, who is otherwise an illiterate or dim wit, does to motivates the youth in Tamil Nadu. It is a form of cult hysteria, a temporary insanity much as a ranting raving ex-corporal of the German army, Adolf Hitler, was able to sway their nation's Nobel Laureates to organize the scientific murder of helpless innocent Jews by the millions.

Pakistan had increasingly sought the support of LTTE to train the terrorists it employs. That need is now being addressed by the LTTE. There are firm reports that the ULFA and other insurgent groups in India's North-East are leaning on new operation techniques. This is coming across in the bomb blasts they are organizing in public places. *This is the first time we are witnessing the phenomenon of outsourcing in terrorism operations.* In 1991 when I was a senior Minister and member of the Cabinet Committee on Political Affairs (CCPA), our Intelligence Agencies had briefed me on the LTTE-ULFA nexus. According to former R&AW official B. Raman, [see his *The Kaoboys of R&AW*], RAW had prepared a dossier on the ISI facilitation of providing weapons to the LTTE by the Harkat-ul-Mujahideen. One ship carrying loads of weapons left Karachi in 1995 with "Kittu" on board. It was interrupted by the Coast Guard. Kittu committed cynonide suicide.

The ISI is seeking to broad-base its sphere of influence and improve the capabilities of terror or insurgent groups. It had been influencing ULFA not to enter into any negotiations with the Indian Government and instead carry out specific attacks. A batch of 15 ULFA cadres were recently sent to Pakistan for advanced training by the LTTE. Many meet ISI agents in Bangladesh, especially in Chittagong area.

ULFA and LTTE have been cooperating since 1990. ULFA has taken LTTE's support for maritime contacts, sea routes because

ULFA also owns a few trawlers operating from Chittagong and it connects them to even Cambodia.

It was the ISI which had introduced ULFA to LTTE transporters who, for a fee, undertook to transport arms from South-East Asia into Myanmar. The LTTE is reported to have trained various ULFA cadres in explosives handling.

The increasing terror activities in south India may have had a link with the ISI-LTTE bond against India. The arrest of two Pakistani terrorists in Mysore a few years ago has unveiled the shifting .base to south India and it has possible link with Colombo. There are reports of ISI presence in Sri Lanka to control the terrorist activities in south India. Bangalore has several defence, atomic and space establishments and is the centre place of India's booming IT sector.

While Pakistan has been officially selling arms to the Sri Lanka Government, ostensibly to assist the latter fight insurgency, the ISI has started a covert supply of arms and other material to the same insurgents, the LTTE rebels, with the clear aim of befriending the terrorist group so that it facilitates its efforts to unleash terror in south and north-east India.

The arrests of some Pakistani terrorists in south India during 2006-10 have heightened speculation about secret links between the ISI and the LTTE. These reports cannot be dismissed lightly because Pakistan, through the ISI, has long been trying to encircle India with bases for subversive, anti-India elements in Nepal, Bangladesh and Sri Lanka. Now in tandem with China which has turned hostile to India, this axis of Pakistan and China, and soon to be augmented by Taliban controlled Afghanistan, is a huge terror threat to India.

Being under the scanner on the western border, the basic objective of the ISI in Bangladesh is the encirclement of India. It uses the strategy of supporting and encouraging insurgency in the north-east with active support from anti-India elements in Bangladesh. The ISI has managed to establish a intricate, network in Bangladesh, due to the presence of pro-Pakistan sympathizers after 1971 and made inroads in Bangladeshi society and polity between the period 1975-96 when the Awami League was out of power. ISI's presence in Bangladesh is with the sole motive of destabilizing India.

Today, the ULFA no longer espouses the ideology of a migrant-free Assam and has even justified the contribution of illegal Bangladeshis in Assam's economy. Contrasting this with the ULFA's original aims and objectives will leave nobody in doubt that it is now completely under the influence of its ISI and Bangladeshi masters. Its original manifesto had justified its creation in 1979 as a fight against the "influx of foreigners and massive exploitation of its natural resources." ULFA's targeting of the innocents is part of the ISI strategy of bleeding India through "a thousand cuts."

The LTTE not only collaborated with the ISI of Pakistan, but in Afghanistan, before 9/11, it worked with Al Qaeda. The LTTE, for example, acquired limited anti-aircraft capability in 1994, when it helped the Harkat-ul-Mujahideen of Pakistan to transport arms and ammunition to the Al Qaeda supported Abu Sayyaf group in Southern Philippines in return for which the Harkat-ul-Mujahideen shared some of the spoils of these arms and ammunition with the LTTE, which included anti-aircraft missiles. This included not only some conventional anti-aircraft missiles but also shoulder-fired missiles. B. Raman, former R&AW official, has opined that the LTTE's stock of ammunition for its conventional anti-aircraft weapons appear to be exhausted and also that possibly the life period of the batteries required to fire the shoulder-fired missiles had also expired and that the LTTE has not be able to replenish its stock. The LTTE, therefore, had no anti-aircraft capability against the Sri Lankan military till recently and hence they were madly in search in India, hoping to bribe some politician–business nexus to make arrangements. It probably succeeded judged by the fact that the Sri Lankan Air Force is unable to bomb on the ground the six micro light-aircrafts that the LTTE has based in Jaffna.

The terror network has also expanded with ISI establishing contacts with Maoists and Islamist NGOs in Nepal to plan and execute anti-India operations, according to Wilson John writing in *Pioneer* news daily on "ISI's new strategy" (14 February 2007). According to Wilson John, the arrest of a Nepalese gun runner in Baramullah early in February 2007 unraveled clues that confirm the expanding network of terror siege in and around India, aided by Pakistan-based terrorist organizations like Lashkar-e-Tayyeba (LeT) and the ISI. Pasang Lama, a resident of Humla district near Kathmandu, has been acting as a conduit between Maoists in Nepal and LeT in Jammu and Kashmir, orchestrated by the ISI which, since the peace process between India and Pakistan began in 2004, has been trying to cobble together a coalition of terror groups targeting India.

The ISI's game plan in Nepal is not new. The difference is in the strategy, which fits in neatly with the overall plan to raise the level of terrorist threat to India without getting Pakistan into the dock. Lama is a tiny cog in this wheel. Lama, who rented out a room in G-49, Vikas Marg, Laxmi Nagar (a low-middle class, crowded locality in East Delhi), worked under the camouflage of a shawl and carpet dealer.

He was a frequent visitor to Jammu and Kashmir and lived, for three months in a year, in Srinagar. His main contact person in Srinagar was a High Court lawyer, Abdul Latif Wani, while in

Delhi, Lama, took orders from Kunjup Tsering who happened to be the gun runner for Maoists. Lama made his money by buying weapons from Kashmiri terrorist groups at cheaper rates and selling it at a higher price to Tsering. The transactions were facilitated through the accounts of Wani in Jammu & Kashmir Bank and Vijaya Bank. Last December, Lama paid Rs. 4,77,000 to buy AK-47 rifles, hand-grenades, rocket launchers and pistols which he delivered to Tsering in a fruit truck. Lama and Tsering have been in the business of gun-running for the past four years. Lama's interrogation revealed that he had more than weapons on his agenda. He was an ISI agent networking with Maoists as well as terrorist groups like LeT establishing not only a conduit for weapons but also for training. He was liaisoning with LeT members to set up joint training camps for making IEDs.

Lama's disclosures are not really surprising. Evidence has been gathering for quite some time about the re-grouping of ISI-backed Muslim outfits, funded by West Asian entities, terrorist groups like LeT in Nepal, specially in the terai region which has been a traditional recruitment and training ground for terrorist groups. Muslims constitute 4.2 per cent of the Nepalese population and of which 96.7 per cent live in the terai region. Almost all the recent terrorist attacks in India—Ayodhya attack of July 2005; Delhi blast of October 2005; Varanasi attack of March 2006; and the Mumbai train serial blasts of July 2006—have Nepal links. LeT operatives, involved in the attacks, have either used Nepal as a transit point between Pakistan and Bangladesh or masterminded terrorist operations in India from Kathmandu and other towns.

Two days after the Mumbai blasts, two Pakistanis, involved in the planning of the attack carried out by LeT, Moiddin Siddiqui and Ghulam Hasan Cheema, were caught from a five-star hotel in Kathmandu. In the huge arms cache caught in Maharashtra early 2006, two months before the Mumbai blast, one of the key operatives caught in the aftermath was Akif Biyabani, an associate of Zahibuddin Ansari alias Zaby, a LeT commander who has planned the operations in Nepal early 2005.

Although Nepal has been known to play host to ISI and its various front organizations, there has been a significant shift in the strategy after 9/11. Instead of operating own units, as it was doing in the past, the ISI has been keen on establishing networks with Maoists and Muslim NGOs to plan and execute anti-India operations. Last November, Nepal Maoist chief Prachanda revealed that the ISI had offered to help his group through "direct or indirect" means.

Some of the NGOs, which are known to be sheltering terrorist groups like LeT in Nepal, include Kashmir Jama Masjid Democratic Muslim Association, Nepal World Islamic Council and Nepal Islamic Yuva Sangh, Jamat-e-Ahle-Hadis, Millet-e-lslami and Jam Seraj-ul Alam. The number of such institutions, according to a recent intelligence report prepared by Sashastra Seema Bal (SSB), could be as high as 73. The report detailed the involvement of ISI (and Pakistani High Commission officials) in using these organizations for anti-India operations.

These organizations are largely funded by charity organizations and banks based in West Asia and Pakistan. There is evidence of the involvement of the Islamic Development Bank (Jeddah) and Habib Bank of Pakistan, which has a partner stake in Nepal's Himalayan Bank, in facilitating the transfer of funds for anti-India activities. The latest report only confirms an earlier report, 'Pakistan's Anti-India Activities in Nepal' (2000), which gave details of ISI's modus operand!, including the use of NGOs and *madarsas* in anti-India operations.

One of the districts where *jihadis* are grouping rapidly is Sunsari where a large number of illegal Bangladeshis have settled in the recent times. The NGO which is active in the area is Nepali Islamic Sangh which is working in tandem with the Bangladesh-based Jamatul Mujahideen Bangladesh (JMB), an associate of Harkat-ul Jihad al Islami (HuJI). HuJI, known as the Bangladeshi Taliban, is an Al Qaeda clone and has been recruiting terrorists in Bangladesh and India. JMB is known as the operational arm of HuJI. As investigations in the terrorist attacks in the last two years in India have shown both HuJI and JMB have aligned with LeT and Students Islamic Movement of India (SIMI) to establish terror networks across India.

CHAPTER V

A Strategy to Deter Terrorism

The quick and unprecedented victory of America-led coalition forces over Iraq and Afghanistan showed that terror-sponsoring Islamic states lack formal military might. However through proxies, the remaining radical Islamic states of the globe have imposed a painful terror war on the US and its allies. Some of the more radical states such as Iran, are even at the threshold of acquiring nuclear weapon capability. By terror tactics, pressure mounted on America, with its military and economic toll more than 2 trillion dollars thus far and over 7,000 civilians and military personnel killed and several tens of thousands injured, to cut and run from Iraq and Afghanistan. Hence, the US has now washed its hands off from Iraq and Afghanistan. Terrorists such as ISIS and Taliban will soon fill the vacuum by 2024. Such an outcome would be worse than British P.M. Neville Chamberlain's capitulation in September 1939 to Hitler. Former US President, George Bush Jr has recently pointed out the most regretable decision of current US President Biden to withdrew from Afghanistan, and in effect handing over that country to Taliban.

An Islamic *jihad* ignored, is not a problem that will go away, because terrorism will stop at nothing less than destruction of democratic civilization. Terrorists have a clear focus: that the sheet-anchor of today's anti-terrorist forces—United States of America—must be brought to its knees; its economic and military capability decimated by attrition.

This and other serious threats are looming large: Europe faces the probability of being "overrun demographically" by Muslims. Israel and India are under a civilizational siege from Islamic terrorists, based on their borders, and subject to continual suicide bombings of innocent civilians. Thus, USA, India and Israel are in the "Focus of *Jihad*."

The bitter truth is that Islamic terrorist's offensive today, represented by the likes of Al-Qaeda, is sustaining due to the clandestine sponsorship by a *de facto* "Axis of *Jihad* " of three nations: Saudi Arabia, Pakistan and Iran. Two of these three nations are close allies of the USA!

Since nuclear bomb-making physics and technology are easily available, even through the Internet, radical Muslim groups embedded in this "Axis" countries can (and will) acquire nuclear bombs. In the not-so-far future thus, America, Israel, and India, the primary targets of Osama Bin Laden's rhetoric, could face nuclear devastation. It is going to require more than conventional military capability to dissuade Muslim radicals from using nukes on these three "Focus of *Jihad*" nations. Hence, how the nations of "Focus of *Jihad*" deter and deal with the "Axis of *Jihad*" nations is crucial for prevention of the nuclear holocaust in the future.

Headway can be made, and success against terror, therefore, achieved effectively going after the "Axis of *Jihad*" nations, and the nodal points of social networks in Muslim communities in this "Axis" that spawn terror, including *Madrassas* and *Masjids.*

We need an innovative multinational anti-terror policy that does not call for direct occupation of *jihad*-sponsoring nations, but executes a counter-offensive against the ideology of "political Islam." It would also call for intensive R&D development by the "Focus of *Jihad*" nations, to develop at the earliest, alternative fuel options such as hydrogen fuel cells to dry up revenue sources of the crude oil producing *jihad*-friendly nations.

India is a nation that has long been ravaged by waves of Muslim invasions, and had been ruled by established Muslim kingdoms (from Akbar's to Aurangzeb's) for 150 years. India is also a nation that was partitioned on the basis of Islam only 75 years ago by the British imperialists. But Islamist radicals regrettably view India as a Hindu nation that escaped total Islamic religious conversion that happened in Iraq, Egypt and Iran. All available evidence points to a concerted and ongoing effort by the ideologues of ISIS and "Caliphate" to "complete the mission" of total Islamic conquest of India, mad as the notion may seem to us today.

The siege of "Hindu India" by political Islam is a subset of the terror war sponsored by the "Axis of *Jihad*" on the "Focus of *Jihad*" nations. Terror in India is intensifying despite the current economic resurgence of the nation. Let us not forget that Islamic onslaught first took place when India was at the height of her prosperity thousand years ago. Today we are economically much weaker state.

Hence, there is a clear need today for us Indians to understand the nature of Islam as a political ideology in the global context; and develop a 'Virat' mindset.

Islam had been an expanding power until at least the 18th century, with a long history of conflict with Christianity, religion of the majority in the West. Islam and Christianity had converted the people of nations that they conquered into nearly 100 per cent Muslims or Christians. *India was the exception* which despite eight hundred years of Islamic and two hundred of Christian conquests has remained overwhelmingly Hindu. This fact has been a living regret for Islamic orthodoxy, while Christian foreign missionaries in India articulate the same regret more subtly. In today's *jihad* contexts, without understanding the nature of Islamic tenets and this history we can never formulate an effective anti-terrorist answer. Correct answers require posing correct questions. The correct question is "What is political Islam and its theological fundamentals?"

Islamic scriptures are divided into "spiritual Islam" and "Political Islam." Islamic trilogy—consisting of the *Koran*, *Hadith* and *Sira*—is the religion. Of this, political Islam is outlined in *Hadith* and *Sira*. Spiritual Islam is what *Koran* preaches. Political Islam, as presented in *Hadith* and *Sira* commands Muslims to conquer the world for Islam. It governs the kind of life and political system to which Muslims should adhere strictly, based on its legal code called *sharia*, an unchanged document that was written over a thousand years ago.

The economic and social aspirations of Muslims and rising expectations of globalization fueled by television and movies from the West conflict with the tenets of the *sharia.* Hence, the religious orthodoxy focusses in their preachings on the Muslim conquest of "unbelievers," or non-Muslims to retain the purity of Islamic culture. There is no room for reform since the *sharia* cannot be questioned. This code *does not* embody a spiritual philosophy, and hence there is no room for debate.

Thus, wherever Muslims felt that they had materially fallen behind, the orthodoxy was called for Muslims to embrace even more retrogressive practices of political Islam. Dr. Muthu Muthuswamy in his *Art of Terror* notes, these practices include literal interpretations of the Islamic trilogy and the importance of conquest through *jihad*, rather than introspection and the reinterpretation of scriptures in a contemporary way, and or the secular downgrading of the importance given to them. The fundamentalists instead assert that once the whole world is Islamized, everyone will feel fulfilled and be at peace with one another. And those Muslims who will willingly die for this cause, including by committing suicide, will go to a "heaven" resembling an Islamic Las Vegas.

Hence, the agenda set by political Islam for believing Muslims is spawning of terrorism and is at the root of it.

The doctrine of *jihad* is the most important tool that political Islam uses to assert its influence and achieve its vision. The term *jihad* in Islamic trilogy describes two concepts: there is *jihad as an inner struggle,* whose aim is to please the almighty God by spiritual purity and then there is *jihad as external warfare,* aimed at conquest of unbelievers and the imposition of Islam on its inhabitants. Armed warfare imposed on unbelievers is one acceptable form of *jihad.* In *Bukhari Hadith,* the most respected of *Hadiths,* 97 per cent of the *jihad* references are about war and only 3 per cent are about the inner spiritual struggle.

Pakistan's orthodoxy, regarding their nation as the torchbearer for Islam in South Asia, sees the largest nation in the region, the Hindu dominant majority India, as the stumbling block for extending Islamic boundaries. Although Sunni-majority Pakistan was frustrated by its smaller size and lack of resources, it has an extensive track record of *jihad* dating back to 1947. Even without Saudi funding, between 1947-1980, Pakistan has been a nation committed to selective killings of non-Muslims or their displacement as part of a *jihad.* Generous *jihad* funding from Saudi Arabia (which is also predominantly Sunni) since the mid-1970s has made Pakistan powerful den of Islamic orthodoxy. The secular urbanized Pakistani community is a wholly marginalized segment of society.

Perhaps more than any other Islamic nation, Pakistan has acted as a collaborator for Saudi Arabian ideologues of Washabism Islam, and a translator of *jihad* plans into action; it has provided logistics, training and know-how for jihadist movements around the world. For instance, financially, aided by Saudi Arabia, the Afghan Taliban was Pakistan's creation.

The Soviet occupation of Islamic Afghanistan was used to build *jihad* fervor in many Islamic nations. The Soviets found the occupation untenable because political Islam was entrenched in the minds of Afghans and because a relentless and resourceful enemy kept coming at Soviet troops from Pakistan. After the Soviet retreat, the Afghan faction called the "Taliban" consolidated power. The Taliban consisted of former students from Pakistani *madarasas* (Muslim religious schools) and was the brainchild of Pakistani intelligence—specifically, the Inter Services Intelligence (ISI). "Talibanization" of Muslim youth is today at the root of anit-Indian terrorism. This is now being repeated when US determination to vacate its troops from Afghanistan.

One unfortunate side product of the Soviet-Afghan war was the modern training in warfare of nationals called Mujahideen, from many Islamic nations, for conducting *jihad.* Upon returning home, many of these *jihadis* set about establishing terror cells with the aim of overthrowing existing governments that they saw as un-Islamic. As a result, instabilities were being created in many Muslim nations, including in Egypt, Saudi Arabia, and Pakistan itself. A band of Arab Islamic radicals, including Osama Bin Laden and his cohorts, decided to stay back in Afghanistan and use it as abase for *jihad* against unbelievers. Thus emerged the Bin Laden's group, Al-Qaeda.

When it quickly became apparent that Al-Qaeda was behind 9/11 attacks, a vastly superior American military invaded Afghanistan and quickly toppled the Taliban and Al-Qaeda from power, with the help of anti-Taliban Northern Alliance. But poor politics, and Pakistan's complicity, allowed the toppled Al-Qaeda and Taliban leadership including the late Osama Bin Laden, to escape to safe sanctuary in neighbouring areas of Pakistan.

However, Bin Laden, Al-Qaeda, the Taliban are sequential symptoms of a resurging political Islamic movement, adhering to Sunni or Shia fundamentals, and nurtured by powerful financial entities in Saudi Arabia, through Hizbollah sponsored by Shitte Iran. *The war on terror therefore has to focus not on the proxies,* like Al-Qaeda, or Hizbullah but on confronting and neutralizing the terrorist nests and incubators in the "Axis of *Jihad*" nations.

The Saudi Government, with the connivance of then Pakistan P. M. Benazir Bhutto, had been the principal financial underwriters of Afghanistan's fundamentalist Taliban movement since 1996. The Taliban not only had strong backing among the public in Pakistan, but ISI was at the forefront of sponsoring and aiding the Taliban. Fuel, arms, ammunition fake currency, and even advice came from Pakistan. The madarasa-educated, semi-illiterate Taliban leadership didn't have the experience in running the nation, so Pakistanis did it for them. When Bahamian Buddhas were blown up by the Afghan Taliban, the expertise was provided by Pakistan and Saudi engineers.

Throughout the nineties, when American targets were being attacked in many parts of the world by Al-Qaeda, most of its members used the Pakistan Port city of Karachi as a transit point to fly in and out of Pakistan and to reach Afghanistan by road. The LTTE in Sri Lanka incidentally had used this facility to mobilize weapons through the sea from Karachi.

Even if Gen. Pervez Musharraf, the then Pakistani President, was personally sincere about ending Pakistan's support for the Taliban, the Establishment in Pakistan—especially the ISI, a deeply political Islam-influenced institution obviously has other ideas. According to Dr. Muthuswamy's study, in December 2006, a captured Taliban spokesman had told Afghan investigators that the Taliban would never have been able to challenge Afghan military and NATO forces without the direct assistance of Pakistan's ISI. This goes to prove that the most influential entity in Islamic Pakistan is political Islam.

Thus, "political" Islam and its core concept of *jihad* have spread throughout the world invigorated by the financial sponsorship of three nations: Saudi Arabia, Iran and Pakistan, the "Axis of *Jihad.*" This axis has a common vision despite other deep differences, viz. conquest of unbelievers and their lands, and the active or complicit sponsorship of terror as a long-standing instrument to further this Islamic vision.

The more secular Islamic states, such as Syria, had originally used terrorism as part of military and foreign policy strategy, *but not as a jihad tool.* But today, in terms ideological commitment, and *jihad-sponsorship,* the "axis" nations are the *de facto* leaders and while other Islamic states such as Syria are willing or reluctant followers.

An article in *The Spectator* (2006) published in London, Stephen Schwartz points out that people who have embraced Sunni Wahhabism have conducted every major terrorist attack against the West in recent years. "Bin Laden is a Wahhabi. So are the suicide bombers in Israel. So are his Egyptian allies, who exulted as they stabbed foreign tourists to death at Luxor.... So are the Algerian terrorists.... So are the Taliban-style guerrillas who murder Hindus in Kashmir..... None of this extremism has been inspired by

American fumbling in the world, and it has little to do with the tragedies that have beset Israelis and Palestinians."

In June 2006, Pew Global Attitudes poll showed that a majority of Muslims in Jordan, Egypt and Nigeria, as well as roughly a third of Muslim residents in France, Spain and Great Britain, felt violence against civilians can be justified in order to defend Islam. Of course, it is left to medieval clerics, who are invariably extremists, to define when and where Islam needs to be defended. Thus, from a practical perspective, this poll indicates that a majority of Muslims in many Muslim nations support terror against non-Muslim civilians. Perhaps, the least enthusiastic about political Islam amongst Muslims are those resident in India. The recent and repeated targeting of Muslims in terrorist bombings, such as in Masjids of Nasik and Hyderabad may be to bring the Muslims of India in line with the tenets of the *Hadith* and *Sira*.

The terrorist outfit, Al-Qaeda, has issued an open warning to India saying that the country should be "ready" to see "a series of terror attacks on Indians," of course targeting Hindus but unconcerned if Muslims too die. In a video issued in July 2007, featuring Adam Yahiye Gadahn—an American Al-Qaeda member, Terrorist said in that video that Indian and American diplomatic missions all over the world are their legitimate targets "We shall continue to target you at home and abroad just as you target us at home and abroad," he added.

He accused India of killing more than a hundred thousand Muslims in Kashmir with "US blessing." The video, one hour and 17 minutes long also has Gadahn warning that President Bush to withdraw his troops from Muslim lands or he can expect worse than September 11. Responding to the threat message by Al-Qaeda junior Home Minister Sri Prakash Jaiswal blandly told the media that "despite reports from the media, we haven't received any official confirmation [sic] regarding the threats. But our country, our paramilitary forces, out security forces are ready to combat any attack of any kind," he added. But earlier, in a *TV 18* network exclusive, National Security Advisor, M. K. Narayanan told Karan Thapar that Al-Qaeda was looking for an opportunity to strike in India and had even done the necessary reconnaissance for it.

"We are concerned. We are all the time on the lookout for Al-Qaeda's movements here. We know that on a couple of occasions they have done a reccee and gone back. But they have not yet done something, which is terrorizing in a big way," he said. Mr. Narayanan also said that the LeT is also an "integral part of al-Qaeda. In a sense you can always say that the al-Qaeda is present in India."

Hence, the blinkers should be cast aside, and we should see the terrorist threat to India, without equivocation and temporizing, as against especially the Hindu civilization. This is the target of Islamic terrorism, and India is being besieged by it and helped by nation-state sponsors abroad as also it's videos within our nation. Our current *defacto* strategy of absorbing the costs of terrorism by an attitude of "business as usual" will simplify not work. *India needs a counter-terror strategy* that deters terrorists from thinking of bleeding our nation, and suffers unbearable costs for terror attacks.

As an essential component of this deterrence strategy, we need a back of adequate constitutionally valid anti-terror legislation, which we lack today.

A number of mature democracies such as the US, UK, France, Germany, Australia, and New Zealand—all with a track record on human rights—have enacted new laws or tightened existing ones to give greater backing to their counter-terror operations (US' record on Guantanamo Bay and Abu Ghraib cannot be cited since these were treated as war camps).

In India, where terror has taken a much bigger toll than in any of these countries, special laws were initially enacted and then withdrawn as they were found to be "draconian." Was that right? Are not special laws for the purposes of fighting terror necessary?

Take New Zealand's example first, after the first flush of concern following 9/11, support for anti-terror laws weakened until Bali massacre happened. Of the 202 dead, three were New Zealanders. The reaction in the island nation to this was swift—Parliament passed the Terrorism Suppression Act with wide support. The law armed agencies to nip extremist organizations and gave them powers to track money trails. In six separate bills, the agencies were empowered to deal with a wide range of offences, including infecting livestock and food contamination.

Wiretaps without warrants in emergency situations were allowed and laws aligned, like use of evidence gathered under one law was allowed to be used against an offence under another law. Any sort of support to terrorism was banned.

In the case of Japan, its Constitution although lays down a pacifist foreign policy agenda, nevertheless the Bill to Respond to Armed Attacks allowed for the first time Japanese forces to consider a pre-emptive strike if the interests and safety of citizens were endangered.

Canada, too, enacted a special law against those who knowingly "either directly or indirectly" provide funds for terror crimes. This has apparently made fund raising for various causes more difficult, a squeeze that LTTE found unbearable and hence it was part of the reason that LTTE crumbled before the Rajapaksa led Sri Lanka.

Canada earlier to 9/11 had no specific terror law. Post 9/11 is set down life imprisonment for those guilty of "instructing" anyone to carry out a terrorist strike and a 10-year jail term for harbouring a terrorist. It did away with the need to demonstrate electronic surveillance as a "measure of last resort" while allowing such surveillance. At the same time, it is viewing the setting up of DNA data banks of criminals and terrorists with favour.

Not surprisingly, these measures, as well as similar measures in Germany, UK, Australia, France and the US, faced strong opposition. The debate over special laws in legislatures and in the public domain have taken note of concerns over curbs on individual and human rights. Most laws have safeguards such as parliamentary oversight and independent reviews. CIA and FBI officials have to present testimonies to congressional committees. But, on balance, collective security has been given precedence. That is why US has enacted the Patriot Act.

In India, in response to a demand for bringing back the Prevention of Terror Act (POTA), it has been argued back that the Terror Act could not prevent the 13/12 attack on Parliament. However, because terrorists are very committed and even if they might strike despite special laws, such laws makes their operations tougher to carry out. It cannot be argued that because murders in ordinary crimes do take place, hence the Indian Penal Code would be scrapped.

Apart from enacting these laws, countries have to integrate laws to allow wiretaps, have doubled or trebled border guards, customs and investigators, enhanced coordination between banks and other financial institutions and regulators, make sharing of data banks easier, introduced video surveillance, mandatory maintenance of telephone records, designation of terrorist crime and, above all, fast trials and tough sentences for the convicted.

In India, the dimension of terror sponsors are many—it has neighbours like Pakistan and Bangladesh, where terror groups like JeM, LeT and HUJI find shelter, and perhaps much more. Besides, there are no racial distinctions between the operatives of these groups and Indians, unlike in western democracies. On top of this, there are pockets in the country which appear to have been influenced by extremist doctrines; thus, it's not as difficult to find logistical support in India as it is in western democracies.

Targeting terrorism through special laws therefore is also a declaration of intent and signals that the political and societal have resolved to take on the terrorist enemy.

Yet in India we are still shying away from doing any of this in the fear that the wider powers given to agencies would be abused. That is not a good enough reason to weaken the battle against terror? Of course we should have special anti-terror laws *and like in other democracies,* make them open to legislative oversight and reviews. That will give our police more of a level playing field against terror.

Since the terrorists threat to India has become multidimensional and complex, the question is whether one can devise a counter-terrorist deterrence strategy. Most prominent national security analysts have argued that deterrent strategies are difficult to formulate and any that is devised will have no significant impact in countering terrorist threat. For example, Richard Betts writes that deterrence has "limited efficacy ... for modern counter-terrorism." The 2002 Rand Corporation study on terrorism asserts, "The concept of deterrence is both too limiting and too naïve to be applicable to the war on terrorism." And the belief that traditional deterrence is inadequate as a counterterrorist strategy is also shared by President George W. Bush and his administration and whose *National Security Strategy* documents state: "Traditional concepts of deterrence will not work against a terrorist enemy."

This overwhelming consensus has now been convincingly challenged by Robert Trager and Desseslava Zagorcheva, two US based scholars in their study.[13]

According to these two scholars, the case *against* the utility of deterrence strategies in counter-terrorist campaigns appears to rest on three pillars. *First,* terrorists are thought to be irrational, and therefore unresponsive to the cost-benefit calculation required for effective deterrence. *Second,* many terrorists are said to be so highly motivated that they are willing to commit suicide for the cause and so not deterred by fear of death or punishment or of anything else. *Third,* even if terrorists were afraid of punishment, they cannot be deterred because they lack a return address, and hence no retaliation can be visited upon them. If terrorists cannot be found, thinking

[13]"Deterring Terrorism – It can be Done," *International Security Journal,* Harvard-MIT, Vol. 30, No. 3, 2006.

of use of force against them, it is contended is useless. Also ineffective are counter-terrorist strategies of Liberals in which is advocated addressing the "root causes," and by "winning hearts and minds" by providing economic packages and promoting human rights, obviously as a long run solution. As John Maynard Keynes had once said of the "long run": "We could be all dead by then."

These above three premises, if valid, signal a terrible danger because terrorists may soon acquire weapons of mass destruction (if they have not already) posing the gravest threat to world order. And if they cannot be deterred then mass destruction of human settlements would be carried out by the terrorists. Jessica Stern, for example, has opined that terrorists or their state sponsors could obtain nuclear and chemical materials from poorly guarded former Soviet facilities as well as the expertise of their underpaid nuclear scientists.[14] The moment is at hand and upon us.

Trager and Zagorcheva have argued that the claim—that deterrence is ineffective against terrorists—is wrong. Their central thesis is that even the most highly motivated terrorists can be deterred by instead holding at risk their political goals, rather than their life, liberty or property.

From a policy perspective, therefore, the ability of a terrorist-targeted nation to put political goals of terrorists at risk stands the best chance deterring and, hence, becomes the most important objective of counter-terrorism policy. But the contours and structure of a counter-terrorism policy, and the selection of instruments for implementation of the policy, has to be nation-specific and terrorist organization-centric. *There cannot, therefore, be a general global strategy of deterrence against terrorism.*

Deterrence in the Context of a Counter-terrorist Strategy

Of course, deterrence is one of several classes of strategies for countering terrorism. Other strategies propounded invoke solving the root

[14]See Stern. J., *The Ultimate Terrorist,* Cambridge, Mass.: Harvard University Press (1999).

causes and problems, which include persuasion (or "winning hearts and minds"), economic aid, democratization, appeasement, and brute military force of search and destroy. In this study, we advocate for India deterrence as our primary strategy. Other strategies mentioned above may be tried as supplementary and secondary, and sequenced properly.

Indeed, deterrence can be achieved by threat of counter-vailing action if a terrorist acts in a certain way, or if he does not act in a certain way. Thomas Schelling, *Arms and Influence* (pp. 70-71), contrasts *deterrence* (the threat to take hostile action *if* the adversary acts) with *compellence* (the threat to take hostile action *unless* the adversary acts). We shall follow this terminology.

Moreover, traditional view of deterrence in strategic studies literature implies the scope for a bargain: that both sides agree to co-operate on a state of affairs that both prefer to alternatives they face. This is game theory the search is called "Nash equilibrium" named after the Nobel Laureate Princeton Professor John Nash. Deterrence, therefore, is not just about making threats: it is also about making offers for good behaviour. Deterrence and compellence is thus about finding the right combination of threat and offer, and we shall apply this principle to countering terrorism in India.

In the case of terrorist menace, because of their ideological and religious beliefs, many terrorists place extreme value on their political objectives relative to other ends (e.g. life and property). For this reason, it appears impossible that a deterrer could hold at risk something personal or of organization of sufficient value to terrorists such that their behavior is affected. Put differently, if the terrorists' motivation is high enough, then even a small probability of a successful operation is sufficient for them, and hence even a high probability of personal or organizational punishment will not deter them. Further, because the interests of terrorists and states seems so opposed, it also appears impossible that the two sides could agree on a state of affairs that both prefer to that in which each does its worst against the other. *Hence, compromise with a terrorist group is not a feasible alternative strategy.*

High levels of motivation often make terrorists highly susceptible to a deterrence strategy that targets their political goals. Highly motivated terrorists, because they hold their political goals dear, are reluctant to run even low-level risks that hurt their political aims. This magnifies the coercive leverage of strategies that target political ends. *Herein thus lies the clue on how to deter terrorism: a strategy to hurt the terrorist's political goals.*

Lexicographic Ordering of Terrorist Preferences

Terrorists are highly irrational by mainstream norms, but not completely. A growing body of literature that shows that terrorist groups (though not necessarily every individual who engages in terrorist activities) usually have lexicographically ordered goals and choose their strategy accordingly. Lexicographic ordering is like words ordered in a dictionary or names in a directory. Entries are ordered by first alphabet, then second, and so on.

A terrorist is motivated lexicographically. If its political goal is not likely to be met by a particular action, it will look no further. If it is, then it will look further at alternatives of actions, targets and weapons.

Thus, terrorists usually have a range of objectives lexicographically ordered in preference. States also have preferences over these same objectives. When the preference orderings of terrorists and states are diametrically opposed then the question of deterrence becomes crucial.

Hence, recognizing that targeting of Hindus is the political goal of the Islamic terrorists, while Muslims of India are largely just passive spectators, but that the foreign patrons of Islamic terrorists are beginning to engage in terrorist acts that could pit Muslims against Hindus in nation-wide conflagration and possible civil war as in Serbia and Bosnia, *hence the first lesson to be learnt from recent history, for tackling terrorism in India is to recognize that the Hindu is the target, and that Muslims of India are being programmed to slide into suicide against Hindus.* The video-tapes in Bihar and in J&K seeking recruits for terrorism against the "US-Israel-India axis" is an indication of this. It is, therefore, to undermine the Hindu psyche and create fear of civil war that terror attacks are organized. And, hence, since the Hindu is the target, Hindus must collectively respond as Hindus against the terrorist and not feel individually isolated, or worse be complacent because he or she is not personally affected. Instead, the attitude should be that if one Hindu is killed merely because he or she is a Hindu, then a bit of every Hindu also dies. This is a necessary part of a *virat* Hindu, an essential mental attitude required in formulating a deterring strategy against a terrorism that is Hindu-centric in its targets.[15]

Therefore, we have to have a collective mindset as Hindus to stand against the terrorist. In this response, Muslims and Christians of India can join the Hindus if they genuinely feel for the Hindu. They cannot, however do so, if they acknowledge what DNA studies of as published in respected journals on Genetics establish, that though they may be Indian Muslims or Christians, their DNA are the same as are of Hindus. It is not easy for them to acknowledge this ancestry even though that is the truth, because the Muslim *Mullah* and Christian Padres would consider it as unacceptable. That realization of Hindu ancestry of minorities, the preachers fear, will also dilute the religious fervour in their faith and thus create a mental option for their possible re-conversion to the Hinduism. Hence, these religious leaders preach hatred and violence against the *Kafir* and the *pagan,* i.e. the Hindu [for example, read Chapter 8, verse 12, of the *Koran*] to keep the faith of their followers. The Islamic terrorist outfits, e.g. the SIMI being the latest, have already resolved

[15]For fuller discussion of the concept of *virat* Hindu, see my *Hindus Under Siege: The Way Out,* Har-Anand, 2006.

that India is *Darul Harab*, and they are committed to make it *Darul Islam*. That makes them free of any moral compunction whatsoever in dealing with Hindus, including their massacre.

But still, if any Muslim or Christian does so acknowledge his or her Hindu legacy, then we Hindus can accept him or her as a part of our society, the *Brihad Hindu Samaj*, which constitutes Hindustan. India that is Hindustan is thus a nation of Hindus and those others whose ancestors are Hindus. This is the true identity of India, known since ages as Hindustan.

Hence, to begin with, any policy to combat terrorism must first begin with requiring each and every Hindu becoming collectively committed, i.e. cultivating a mindset befitting a virat Hindu. By this is meant that it is not enough commitment if one individually claims to be Hindu, or goes to temples, does *pujas*, and celebrates festivals. That is not sufficient to be a committed or *virat* Hindu. *To be a virat Hindu one must have a Hindu mindset.*[16]

The second lesson for combating the terrorism that we face today is: since demoralizing the Hindu and undermining the Hindu foundation of India in order to destroy the Hindu civilization, is the political goal of terrorists in India we must never capitulate and never concede any demand of the terrorists because that would encourage them further. The release of three hard-core terrorists from jail in December 1999, including Mohammed Azhar of Jaish-e-Mohammed, for release of hijacked *Indian Airlines* passengers in Kandahar, in Afghanistan is a example of such a disastrous capitulation.

Terrorists are encouraged by appeasement but never satisfied by it. Therefore, no matter how many Hindus have to die for it, *the basic policy has to be: never yield to any demand, however, small of the terrorists.* That necessary resolve has not been shown in our recent history. Instead ever since we conceded Pakistan in 1947 under

[16] *Op. cit., Hindus Under Siege.*

duress, we have been mostly yielding time and time again to threats and violence.

In 1989, to obtain the release of Mufti Mohammed Sayeed's daughter, Rubaiyya, who had been kidnapped by terrorists, five terrorists in Indian jails were set free by the V. P. Singh's government. This made these criminals in the eyes of Kashmiri separatists and fence-sitters as heroes, as those who had brought India's "Hindu establishment" on it's knees. To save Rubaiyya, it was not necessary to surrender to terrorist demands. There were other ways. But the then government were of capitulationists in outlook, they did not explore them.

In 1991, when Chandrashekhar was PM, and I was his senior Minister also handling the Law and Justice portfolio, the former Water Resources Minister at the Centre, Saifuddin Soz's daughter, was similarly kidnapped by the JKLF. They too made the same demand [release of four terrorists in jail] but we refused. We also took some secret retaliatory action which frightened the JKLF and hence Soz's daughter was put on a auto-rickshaw and sent home unharmed within two days of our counter-threat that which would have set back their political aims. This toughness was shown at a time when our government was tottering and about to fall! The difference with the V. P. Singh's government was thus in Chandrashekhar government's mindset: it had become clear from day one to the JKLF that we meant business as also that two can play the game.

We also showed similar grit and guts when we received information that LTTE had established a parallel establishment in Tamil Nadu, with the Chief Minister Karunanidhi's connivance. Most of the senior bureaucrats of our government had warned the Prime Minister and me in the Cabinet sub-committee [the CCPA] meeting, that we risked bloodshed and rise of separatist Dravidian movement by taking precipitate action. But we, nevertheless, dismissed the DMK government, sacked the Governor for his inaction, and smashed the terror infrastructure in the state. The people responded by subsequently voting out the DMK in the ensuing polls. Out of 234 Assembly seats, the DMK won just two!! Had we not acted that then, Tamil Nadu would have been worse today than even Kashmir. Thus innate toughness on both occasion was rewarded because we targeted the political goals of the terrorists. The LTTE lost politically because the DMK infrastructure was unavailable thereafter for their India-based activities.

The worst capitulation to terrorists in our modern history was in the *Indian Airlines* hijack incident in December end 1999. The terrorists after hijacking an *Indian Airlines* flight from Kathmandu to Delhi demanded money and release of three of the most dreaded terrorists held in judicial custody in Jammu jail [Maulana Masood Azhar, Omar Sheikh, and Ahmed Zargar]. About 40 policepersons had earlier died in various encounters to capture them. Yet in the call of saving the lives of 259 passengers in the *IA Airbus* parked in Kandhahar, the government released these terrorists even without getting Court permission [required since they were in judicial custody]. They were "released" on 30 December 1999. But the Court having judicial custody was informed only on 3 January 2000 and the Court upheld the *fait accompli* on 29 January 2000 after passing structures. Moreover, the terrorists were escorted by a senior Minister on the PM's special *Boeing* all the way to Kandhahar as royal guests instead of being shoved across the Indo-Pakistan border.

Worse still, all the three after being freed, went back to Pakistan and created three separate terrorist organizations to kill Hindus. Mohammed Azhar, whom the National Security Adviser Brijesh Mishra had then described [on NDTV] as "a mere harmless cleric," upon his release led the Jaish-e-Mohammed to savage and repeated terrorists attacks on Hindus all over India from Bangalore to Srinagar. Since mid-2000, Azhar is responsible for killing of over

3,000 Hindus and also the 2001 attack on India's Parliament. Omar Sheikh is in jail for killing US journalist Daniel Pearl and is in US custody, while the third, Zargar, is engaged today in random killings of Hindus in Doda and Jammu through his Lashkar-e-Jingan.

What should India have done instead? In the first place, it is a mystery how the *IA* plane shrewdly brought by the pilots to land in Amritsar was allowed to take-off again. That was a missed chance which counter-hijack experts find inexplicable. Who was responsible for allowing the plane to take-off? At very least, the tyres of the plane should have been punctured by the NSG present at the airport, positioned with long-range rifles to immobilize the aircraft. A future government ought to inquire into this matter and fix responsibility.

The then Foreign Minister Jaswant Singh, who has written about this in this memoirs, told me that the main motivation in yielding to the hijackers' demand was the seeming collapse of civil society, especially the relatives of the passengers. His government was being counselled to save the lives of the passengers whatever the cost, while hardly any wanted the 'no deal with terrorist' taken. Even the Congress Party in opposition had favoured capitulation.

Nevertheless, the cost paid could have been minimized if [when the plane had landed in Kandahar] the Indian Government had threatened to take counter ground action if any of the passengers had been harmed by the hijackers. This was the suggestion I had publicly made then but the government seemed to have lost its nerve by then, by its apparent lack of support from civil society (was it an excuse) and ready to capitulate. At the very least, we should have demanded the custody of the killer of Rupa Katyal's husband. Who was a passenger on honeymoon with his newly wed wife, Rupa. His throat was slit by one of the hijackers in front of his newly wed wife. The Katyals were returning by the ill-fated flight after their honeymoon in Nepal. Even if all the 259 passengers had to be put at risk, we should have at least demanded that this callous butcher of Katyal be handed over as part of the deal. For freeing Azhar, the Taliban would have sacrificed him. But at the end of it all, Bharat Mata is still bleeding unavenged because Azhar and the two other terrorists went to Pakistan after the unholy swap, and founded terrorist organizations that have, since the year 2000, killed 3,000 innocent citizens. The killing continues even today, with no obvious end in sight. This whole Kandhahar episode proves that we should never negotiate with terrorists and *never yield*. If you do, then sooner or later you will end up losing more lives than you will ever save by a deal with terrorists. Civil society can only be as tough as its politicians, a dictum brought clearly during World War II between the approaches of Neville Chamberlain and Winston Churchill.

The *third lesson to be learnt is that whatever and however small the terrorist incident, the* nation *must retaliate*—nor by *measured and "sober" responses, but by massive retaliation.* For example, when Ayodhya Temple was sought to be attacked, or the Institute of Science in Bangalore was targeted, these were not big terrorist incidents but we should have massively retaliated. Our intelligence agencies also keep telling me in private that we have clinching proof of terrorist training camps in PoK and Bangladesh, and if that is so, we should bomb them by despatching our Air Force. There is some corroborating evidence for the existence of such camps, for example, the US agency, the FBI has evidence which was presented to a district court in California during the trial in 2006 of suspected Pakistani-trained terrorists. Satellite photos with the FBI establish that terror training camps do exist in and around Balakot in northeast Pakistan. Indian Government also claims proof, which has not been made public, that there are 57 camps in Pakistani-held territory and 36 camps in Bangladesh.

If instead of being supportive, Pakistan and Bangladesh protest or retaliate if India bombs these camps, then it means that they are sponsors and not unwilling hosts to freelancing terrorists, and hence we should be ready for war. We could retaliate then by demanding the return of Northern Areas in Karakoram bordering PoK, presently centrally administered by Islamabad. It is good that in the present negotiations for peace in Kashmir, with Pakistan, India has now made clear that Northern Areas are a part of Kashmir, and not part of Pakistan, even if centrally administered by Islamabad.

What should be our measured retaliatory response to terrorist attacks, viz. our strategy to deter terrorists? It is argued by secular "liberals" that *no retaliation against terrorists can be effective because of the high motivation of terrorists.*

What motivates the Islamic terrorists in India? Many "liberals" are advising us Hindus to deal with the root "cause" of terrorism rather than concentrating on eradicating terrorists by retaliation. And pray what is the root "cause"?

According to bleeding-heart liberals, terrorists are born or bred because of four disabilities: *illiteracy, poverty, oppression,* and *discrimination.* They argue that instead of eliminating them which they consider impossible, the root cause of these four disabilities in society should be removed. Only then terrorism will disappear. Moreover they argue, terrorists cannot be deterred by force since they are irrational, willing to commit suicide, and have no "return address." Before replying to this point of view of the liberals, let us understand that I have serious doubts about the integrity of these liberals, or more appropriately, these promiscuous intellectuals. They seek to deaden the emotive power of the individual and render him passive. A nation state cannot survive for long with such a capitulationist mentality. A world survey of Muslims, the largest ever conducted, shows an extraordinarily high proportion of

Muslims outside India supporting *Jihad* and its consequence—terrorism. It is not of ignorance or illiteracy that is motivating terrorists of the Islamic faith. In fact, Islam as a theology is supportive of such extreme violence in its concepts of *Darul Harab, Kafir, Jehad,* and *Dhimmi*. That is why even Muslim majority pockets in Hindu majority (83 per cent) India, have no secularism. Hindus are persecuted in these pockets which we ignore because of the vote-bank politics. One has to visit Kashmir, Meerut, Mau in U.P., Melvishararam and Thondi in Tamil Nadu to see this first hand. It has nothing to do with poverty, illiteracy or unemployment. It is centrally connected with the concepts of Darul Islam and Darul Harab, and the duality in Muslim outlook between when in majority and when in minority.

Searching the backgrounds of some of the world's most notorious Muslim terrorists, the aforementioned Gallup survey of 2005 found that the liberal explanation of four disabilities as the motivator of terrorism as false because:

- Late Bin Laden, the son of a Saudi billionaire, studied engineering.
- His deputy Ayman al-Zawahri was an eye surgeon.
- Mohamed Atta, the son of a lawyer, earned a master's degree in urban planning.
- 9/11 mastermind Khalid Sheikh Mohammed graduated from an American college with an engineering degree.
- Flight 93 pilot Ziad Jarrah's father is a Beirut bureaucrat who drove a Mercedes and put his son through prep school.

Some of the London bombers had college degrees. One was a school teacher. Another's father owned a store.

Many of the Saudi hijackers were the best and brightest in their towns. Hani Hanjour, who crashed the plane into the Pentagon, studied English at the University of Arizona. Family members were wealthy merchants from Taif, a resort city in Saudi Arabia.

Most Palestinian suicide bombers have come from middle-class homes. They didn't do what they did to escape poverty.

And some of the most radical imams in America have doctorates.

This Gallup's survey of Muslims, the largest conducted, puts to rest theories that Islamic terrorists attack because they are poor and alienated from society. Or because they are dim and easily misled.

Muslim fundamentalists have an education and an economic future, yet they still terrorize and hate. They are literate enough to liberally interpret their holy books, yet they still embrace *Jihad* against *Kafirs*, and revel in obscurantism and violence.

The fourth lesson to learn is that more than the overt threat of the terrorists in India, the more sinister corrosion of our nation state occurs from within. This corrosion provides "a force multiplier" to the terrorists. That is, the terrorists are able to leverage the influence of highly placed individuals in the government, media and academia, who have been compromised by the terrorists and blackmailed on sex, drug money and illegitimate favours, into collaborating with them. Take for example the assassination of Rajiv Gandhi. He had been the Prime Minister, and the LTTE killed him because it claimed that he had to be punished for sending the IPKF to Sri Lanka. The dispatch of the Indian army was a government policy ratified by Parliament, and yet the LTTE, a foreign terrorist organization, arrogated to itself the right to hold Rajiv Gandhi responsible and to be murdered for it. In other words, the assassination of Rajiv Gandhi was LTTE's challenge to India's sovereignty and self-respect itself, in that a foreign terrorist organization can decide to kill because it does not like a policy of the Government of India. Incidentally and surprisingly, the LTTE itself was a party to the decision to send the IPKF, but found soon enough that Indian Army was not going to do the LTTE's dirty work and hand over Eelam to them on a platter. So they turned against India. So, it was their perfidy that needs punishing.

But instead of revulsion against the LTTE that any Indian patriot in government, media or academia would feel, we find that there are political parties, which have no shame in stating that Rajiv Gandhi deserved to die. More surprisingly, the Congress Party finds nothing wrong with having political alliances with such parties. Furthermore, Ms. Sonia Gandhi, the widow of the martyred Rajiv Gandhi made an appeal to the President that the four LTTE criminals, to be hanged on the orders of the Supreme Court [delivered on 12 May 1999], *should be given a lesser sentence of life imprisonment* even though the four criminals did not ask for mercy! Is this their concept of zero tolerance for terrorism, or is there some mysterious hidden reason? And why is it that ever since the assassination, and till today, no single letter has been written to the President or no demand has been raised in Lok Sabha then for the immediate extradition of the LTTE supremo and Accused no. 1 in the Rajiv murder case, V. Prabhakaran, or even carpet bombing of his hideout in Mullaitheevu or wherever in Sri Lanka? Even the media and the academia did not write op-ed pages demanding action. Why did not the media raise this question of alliance of Congress with pro-LTTE parties? What is behind this conspiracy of silence? One thing is for sure—terrorists in India of all hues and background have their compromised moles in the India's Establishment, and hence no anti-terrorist policy can succeed unless these fifth column elements are weeded out. The IB/RAW/MI/CRPF all have files on them and so identifying them is no problem. But this would a major revamp of these agencies for them to become the cutting edge of our anti-terrorist policies.

A succinct overview on India's response to terrorism to date has been provided by Tarun Vijay, Editor of *Panchjanya Weekly.* Writing in *Times of India* (26 August 2007) he stated:

Terror is sought to be countered with "band-aid fixes." And he queries: "How to transform the "band-aid state" into a collective resolve to counter-terror?"

He argues: "Because terrorists bombs do not arrive uninvited. They are in fact invited and sheltered and facilitated." The biggest facilitation, he forcefully argues, comes from the state apparatus through the creation of an atmosphere where blasts become a routine affair. So much so that people stop counting or reacting to them. The blasts, the condemnations, the expression of deep sorrows and the firm resolves—"not to be cowed down by such dastardly acts" become so standardized like the cyclostyled copies of the municipal payment receipts we used to see in childhood days, that nobody read." Never eliminating the cause of the hurt, never finding the permanent solutions. Just a first-aid and the matter ends like an ill-equipped public hospital treating a wounded pedestrian. Recently, several thousand Bangladeshi Muslim infiltrators were caught by the Arunachal Pradesh government and thrown out of the state immediately, the All-Assam Minorities Students Union, Assam, issued a warning that unless they are "accommodated," they will push out all Assamese (read Hindus) from three Muslim-dominated districts of Assam—Dhubri, Goalpara and Barpeta. In no time Assam's Chief Minister issued a statement that all of these Muslims, ousted by the Arunachal Government, belong to Barpeta and so shall be accommodated there. There was no enquiry that on what basis the Arunachal Government has declared these people as Bangladeshis and unless the matter is settled between two Indian provinces, nothing decisive should be spoken for those declared aliens. The Central government maintained a studied silence.

In Assam, the prevailing perception is that any Bangladeshi can claim or her citizenship to Barpeta, because it's a city run and controlled by Bangladeshi illegal infiltrators.

Assam is the only place on this earth where a native government enacted a foreigners' registration act *which puts the onus of proving a person's nationality* on the police or the complainant rather than on the suspect! It was known as the illegal Migrants (Determination by Tribunals) Act (1983) applicable to one state only so that in effect Bangladeshi illegal infiltrators are facilitated to sneak in.

A nation living on a self-denial mode can never defeat gun culture. "Band-aid" prescriptions and similar analyses are of no use unless the real spirit of the nation is recognized and nourished.

It is also a ridiculous idea that terrorists cannot be deterred because they are irrational, willing to die, and have no "return address." Our inference here is that the terrorist master-minds have political goals and a method in their madness. *An effective strategy to deter terrorism is, therefore, to defeat those political goals and to rubbish them by counter-terrorist action.* What that is for India, we shall explore below.

A Strategy of Deterrence Against Terrorism

Applying these principles, I advocate the following strategy to negate the political goals of Islamic terrorism in India, and thus deter these terrorists from engaging in violent behaviour. What are these political goals that have to be frustrated for the terrorists? Below I list a few:

Terrorist Goal #1: Overawe India on Kashmir by incessant terrorist violence and killings, to agree to part with that state.

Counter-Strategy: Removed Article 370 by a Presidential Notification in 2019, but the Government is yet to resettle one million ex-servicemen in the Valley to maintain Hindu Muslim peace and unity to enable the Kashmiri Hindus and Sikhs to return to their homes in the Kashmir Valley. For this it is essential to create closed Kashmiri conclaves for the Hindu Pandit and Sikh communities of 500,000 who are presently displaced or as refugees elsewhere. If Islamic terrorists continue to come across the Line of Control in Kashmir and create disorder and murder, then India must search for an opportunity to take over PoK. If Pakistan either fails to block, or worse continues to back terrorists, then assist the Balochis and Sindhis to struggle for independence. The Balochis were anyway never legally merged into Pakistan. It was a conspiracy of silence on the part of Congress leadership that Balochistan is today a part of Pakistan.

In 1893, the Afghan and British governments had agreed to demarcate a 2,500 kilometer long border to divide British India from Afghanistan. The signatories of the "Durand Line" Agreement, were Amir Abdur Rahman Khan, ruler of Afghanistan, and Sir Henry Mortimer Durand, the then foreign secretary of the British Indian Government. After a series of battles and treaties signed by the British, "The Durand Line Agreement" of 1893 divided the boundaries between three sovereign countries, namely, Afghanistan, Balochistan and British India. The agreement should have been a trilateral one and it legally required the participation and signatures of all three sovereign countries. However, the clever British had drawn the agreement bilaterally between Afghanistan and British India only, and it intentionally excluded Balochistan. According to that agreement, the British imperialists had leased out for themselves the N.W. F. P. and Balochistan, without the knowledge of Balochistan. Sir Durand gave verbal assurance to Afghanistan that the lease will last a hundred years, until 1993, but in the agreement there is no mention of the time limit. Otherwise, just like Hong Kong, N.W.F.P., for example, should have been gone back to Afghanistan in 1993. Balochistan should have become an independent country in 1947 after paramountcy of Britain ended.

However, in 1949, Afghanistan's "Loya Jirga" (Grand Council) declared the Durand Line Agreement itself as invalid, and also raised objections in the United Nations.

International law states that boundary changes must be made among all concerned parties; a unilateral declaration by one party has no legitimacy. However, the British Government disregarding the objection of Afghanistan gave away the N.W.F.P. to Pakistan after a contrived "plebscite." However, it never ceded Balochistan to Pakistan in a legal way.

Throughout the period of British rule of India, the British never occupied Balochistan. There were treaties and lease agreements between the two sovereign states, but neither state invaded the other. Although the treaties signed between British India and Balochistan provided many concessions to the British, but none of the treaties permitted the British to demarcate the boundaries of Balochistan without the consent of the Baluch rulers.

In fact, on August 11, 1947, the Indian Independence Act passed by British Parliament formally vested control of Balochistan to the Ruler of Balochistan, Mir Ahmad Yar Khan—the Khan of Kalat. The Khan immediately declared himself as sovereign of Balochistan. Mohammad Ali Jinnah accepted the proclamation of Balochistan's sovereignty under the Khan.

The New York Times reported on 12 August 1947: "Under the Agreement, Pakistan recognizes Kalat as an independent sovereign state with a status different from that of the Indian States. "The NY Times" *even printed a map of the world* showing Balochistan as a fully independent country.

Hence, on 15 August 1947 the Khan of Kalat addressed a large gathering in Kalat and formally declared the full independence of Balochistan, and proclaimed the 15th day of August a day of celebration. The Khan also formed the lower and upper house of Kalat Assembly and during the first meeting of the Lower House in early September 1947, the Assembly ratified the declaration of Independence of Balochistan. The Pakistan army, however, invaded Balochistan on 15 April 1948, and imprisoned all members of the Kalat Assembly. India did not protest. Lord Mountbatten as well as Nehru said nothing about the illegal annexation of Balochistan, or later of N.W.F.P. This was the conspiracy of silence and betrayal of India's national interests.

Since, then, Pakistan is nervous of any move that could bring Afghanistan and India together, or suspects any rebellion in Balochistan as an opportunity for India to liberate the annexed nation, much as Bangladesh was with much less legitimacy or basis.

Thus the bottom-line of any interaction with Pakistan has to be that if they do not cooperate with us on annihilating terrorism, then we shall seek to put Pakistan asunder. We shall then do unto them what they have been doing to us so far.

Terrorist Goal #2: Make India into *Darul Islam*. If this is not possible for terrorists in one stroke, make in every pocket where Muslims are in majority, e.g. Kashmir, Mau in U.P., Melvisharam in Vellore, Tamilnadu, etc. to become a mini Darul Islam.

Counter-Strategy: Implement Uniform Civil Code as mandated by Art 44 the Constitution; make Sanskrit learning compulsory and singing of *Vande Mataram* mandatory; and declare India's identity as Hindustan, i.e. as a nation of Hindus and those others whose ancestors are Hindus.

Terrorist-Goal #3: Change India's demography by illegal immigration, conversion, and refusal to adopt family planning.

Counter-Strategy: Enact a national law prohibiting conversion from Hindu religion to any other religion. Re-conversion to Hinduism will not be banned. Declare caste is not birth-based but as Bhagwat Gita mandates, as a code of discipline based on occupation. Welcome non-Hindus to re-convert and treat them as "Ghar Wapasi". Annex Bangla Desh territory of Bangladesh in proportion to the ratio of illegal migrants to total population of that country. At present, northern one-third of Bangladesh from Sylhet to Khulna should be annexed, since the total Bangladeshi illegal immigrants are about one-third of that country's population. Pakistan was conceptually created for those Muslims who could not bear to live with Hindus in India. Hence, if now Muslims cannot bear to live in Bangladesh, we must carve out and return territory in proportion to the illegal migrants. Otherwise, Bangladesh should stop illegal migration into India, and take back those already in India areas illegally.

Terrorist-Goal #4: Denigrate Hinduism through vulgar writings and preaching in Mosques, *Madrassas*, and Churches to create loss of self-respect amongst Hindus and thus mentally fit for capitulation.

Counter-Strategy: Propagate the development of a Hindu mindset[17] and unite Hindus on that basis. Challenge Christians to debate whether Jesus Christ was a Buddhist having been educated and trained in Hemis Gompa near Leh in Ladakh, and buried in Khaniyur near Srinagar along with his wife Mary Magdalen. Ask Muslims if it not a fact that Mecca's Kaaba is originally the site of a Hindu temple, and that all ancient monuments created in India from Babar onwards are based on the Hindus Shilpa Shastra in its floor plan, or built on after demolishing Hindu hoary structures such as temples. In other words, tit for tat. Terror mentality cannot be countered by persuasion but by challenging the basic premises.

India can solve its terrorist problem by such a deterrent strategy, but for that we have to learn the four lessons outlined above, and have a Hindu mindset to take bold, risky, and hard decisions to defend the nation. Terrorists target is Hindu society and its unity. Hence arguments against terrorism cannot be by rebuttal but by counter examples. If the Jews can be transformed from lambs walking meekly to the gas chambers, to fiery lions in just ten years, it is not difficult for Hindus in much better circumstances [after all we have a country of our own to begin with, and are today 82 per cent of India], to do so in five years. Guru Gobind Singh has shown us the way already, how just five fearless persons under spiritual guidance can transform society. The Vijayanagaram empire was founded by two re-converted [from Islam] persons Bukka and Hakka under the spititual guidance of Shankaracharya of Sringeri. So did

[17] *Ibid.*

Krishnadevaraya, Rana Pratap, Shivaji, Rani Jhansi, Kattaboman, and Netaji Subhash Bose inspire the nation to greatness. But since 1947 and so far we Hindus have meekly followed the so-called Nehru's secular principles and which has spiritually, culturally and mentally castrated the nation of Hindustan.

But this mindset of never to capitulate to terrorists, and to retaliate massively to retard the terrorists political goals, requires effective communication in the form of what Harvard scholar T. C. Schelling called as "Compellence." Deterrence and Compellence are two legs on which a nation's security will stand.

Ever since Schelling wrote his seminal book *Arms and Influence* in 1966, most authors[18] have chosen to define compellence by different names including "coercive diplomacy," "force without war," "strategic coercion," "military coercion," "coercive military strategy." We need to distinguish compellence from other uses of military power.

Deterrence and compellence require use threats of force to influence the behaviour of a target.[19] Quoting George and Smoke, "[T]he deterrent use of force is the deployment of military power so as to be able to prevent an adversary from doing something that one does not want him to do and that he might otherwise be tempted to do by threatening him with unacceptable punishment if he does it." The effectiveness of the deterrence depends upon a state's ability to convince a potential adversary that it has both the *will* and the *power* to punish him severely if he undertakes the undesirable action in question.

Compellence is thus a politico-military strategy of using armed forces, the actual engagement of military forces to substantially degrade the terrorist capacity to resist, or inflict damage.

[18]See an excellent review by Wg. Cdr. V. Krishnappa: "Compellence: What is it?" *IDSA* (2006).

[19]Alexander L George and Richard Smoke, *Deterrence in American Foreign Policy: Theory and Practice,* Columbia University Press, New York, 1974.

Compellence requires effective communications, of a process wherein the target nation informs the terrorist outfit of what it wants and what it plans to do if the outfit does not comply and, alternatively, if it does comply, and most important is explicit about the penalties it will apply for non-compliance, and is definite about how it will react if the terrorist outfit does not go along. Compellence is more complex than deterrence because they require affirmative action on the part of the terrorist.

With deterrence and compellence firmly structured in our counter-terrorist policy, we could consider cutting the ground from under the main terrorist outfits of the Islamic fundamentalists *by providing Pakistan a face-saving alternative on a Kashmir settlement.* Indo-Pakistan relations could be founded on it. Armed with a deterrence policy of dismemberment of Pakistan, we should also have a policy of compellence to persuade that nation to come on board as a partner in South Asia. Is it possible to develop such a healthy harmonious relation with Pakistan?

Indo-Pakistan relations have had many ups and down, but mostly down. The ups were during the Janata Party governments, viz. two and half years (1977-79) of Morarji Desai's and seven months (1990-91) of Chandrashekhar's and also during the five years (1991-96) of Narasimha Rao-led Congress government. But during the tenure of other Congress governments as well as in the present BJP-led NDA government period, the relations have been fluctuating with interregnums of extreme hostility, even war (four in the last 56 years), or waxing eloquent about peace and harmony between neighbours.

It will not be an oversimplification to state that the lack of normal healthy and stable Indo-Pakistan relations is mainly due to the unresolved Kashmir issue. Cross-border terrorism, which is being raised by the Indian Government in every forum, is also embedded in the larger Kashmir problem. The former cannot be sustained without the rhetoric on the latter.

Can a genuine thaw in Indo-Pakistan relations happen?

It will require extraordinary effort to find such a solution. There is *prima facie* a doubt if indeed such a solution is practical or operational terms exist at all to be negotiated.

The Kashmir issue is such that for either country there are no solutions achievable by and through compensatory trade-offs with other rewards such as more trade or foreign investments, etc.. People of both countries are emotional about the Kashmir issue. Pakistanis refer to the issue as the "unfinished agenda of Partition" of the Indian subcontinent and crucial to the *raison d'etre* of their nationhood itself. Indians treat it as an Islamic conspiracy to destabilize, to further partition and balkanize the Hindu country. Wasted decades since 1947 have fortified these hard emotions. It is within India's capability today to unravel the residual Pakistan into four separate countries of Baluchistan, Sindh, Pakhtoonistan, and West Punjab.

Pakistan has been unable to keep its national integrity. In 1971, it broke up, and 55 per cent of Pakistan seceded to form Bangladesh. It could easily with Indian assistance break into four, as Yugoslavia did on ethnic grounds.

A further legal dimension arises in the Constitution of India adopted by Indian Parliament in 1950. It does not provide for ceding any territory under any circumstances. Merger into India is a one-way ticket. By the Indian Independence Act, 1947 (from which the new nation of Pakistan draws its own legitimacy) and the Indian Constitution, once the Instrument of Accession was signed by the Maharaja of Kashmir in favor of India, there remained no legal claim of any other nation or peoples, to any part of Kashmir. In this, legally speaking, even the people of Kashmir have no voice. Also Article 103 of the UN Charter has no application here since the Instrument of Accession is not a treaty but a part of the statute that created Pakistan out of an undivided India. Nor does the relevant or any of the UN Resolutions recognize any right of the people of Kashmir, except the right to decide in a plebiscite whether to be a part of India or of Pakistan. There is no third alternative proposed in the Resolutions.

Following the 1947 merger of Kashmir with India, India had recovered two-thirds of Kashmir after sending troops with the intention to clear the Pakistan Army, and before the UN mandated ceasefire, from the whole of Kashmir. Subsequently, in the late 1950s, India lost half of that area to China when the PLA built a highway through Aksai Chin connecting Tibet with Sinkiang. By the time India woke up to it, or took notice of it, it was too late—the road had been built and PLA vehicles were traversing to and fro. The war with China in 1962 made it amply clear that China has no intention to clear out from Aksai Chin. Thus today, of the total area of Kashmir, India, Pakistan and China have a third each under their control. Since 2013, Chinese troops have clandestinely encroached and occupied Indian territory in Ladakh.

Paradoxically, despite a conclusive legal basis for the India's claim to Kashmir, the Indian Government has inexplicably diluted its case on Kashmir by acknowledging that it was a "dispute" between India and Pakistan. This was admitted by India first in the United Nations in 1948. The UN Commission on India and Pakistan (UNCIP) Resolution of 5 January 1949 that limits the proposed plebiscite choice only to accession to either India or Pakistan—and not independence for Kashmir—makes Pakistan the sole alternative party to the dispute. Since then, in the Simla Pact (1972) and the recent Agra Indo-Pak Summit (2001) India has reaffirmed this UN-given status to Pakistan in the Kashmir dispute.

Even in the Indian Constitution, Article 370 clearly implied that Kashmir's merger with India is incomplete and yet unresolved. It was however inserted in the Constitution as a "Temporary" provision. Thus, though India had had an impeccable legal claim to Kashmir, she had lost the moral right to insist on it because of the acceptance by the Indian Government of Kashmir as a disputed state (in which Pakistan is a party) as also by the oft-stated commitment of India to resolve the question by peaceful negotiations with Pakistan. The legal dimension has thus been gravely weakened by past governments and cannot be re-focussed on again—unless the UN resolutions are formally laid to rest or disowned by a future Indian Government. However, there is a ray of hope: In August 2019, the Parliament of India amend out Art. 370 of the Constitution by accepting the Presidential Notification as per Article 370, declaring that the temporary provision of the said Article 370 is deleted.

(*b*) *The second dimension is a moral one* that arises from the universal concept of self-determination that is incorporated in the UN Charter. The United Nations Security Council had considered the Kashmir question because when Nehru was Prime Minister, India originally took the matter to the UN. Pakistan later had also lodged a complaint with UNSC on the issue. Nehru did not have his Cabinet's approval for seeking UN intervention, but not even subsequent Indian Governments have disowned Nehru on this score.

The UN had, upon receiving India's plea, constituted a special mediatory commission (UNCIP) which passed several Resolutions with the prior consent of the two countries. Two of these resolutions are important—the Cease-Fire Proposal Resolution of 13 August 1948 and the Affirming Resolution of 5 January 1949. These two Resolutions are the foundation of the call for a plebiscite that is often made internationally, and to which resolutions both India and Pakistan were willing parties (it is recorded as such in the second Resolution).

It is wrong, to make out that India is unconditionally committed to holding a plebiscite under UN auspices in Kashmir. India is a party to the above-mentioned two Resolutions which together may be called the Plebiscite Resolutions of UNCIP. These two Resolutions (designated here as PR (1948) and PR (1949)) are composite and contain a number of pre-conditions on which the holding of a plebiscite is contingent. Those pre-conditions that devolve on Pakistan have never been met, and it is doubtful if Pakistan can ever meet the commitments without an internal upheaval. For example, Part II (A) Clause 1 of PR (1948) states that "... the Government of Pakistan agrees to withdraw its troops from that state." Part II (A) Clause 2 amplifies this withdrawal to include Pakistani irregulars as well. It is doubtful if any government of Pakistan can carry out these commitments and survive. If it could not be done in 1948, it certainly cannot be done now. The Clauses {Part II (B) Clause 1 read with Clause 4 (a) of PR(1949)} moreover require to be implemented by Pakistan prior to India taking any steps or for the UN to schedule a plebiscite.

Hence, the attempt to portray India as a country that has gone back on its international commitment to hold a plebiscite under UN auspices is simply not true: instead, the UN Resolutions on plebiscite have by now become dead letters because none of the conditions precedent for its implementation obtain. Nor, I would guess would Pakistan even today be able to meet those conditions— constrained as it is by domestic compulsions. That is, self-determination, not being an abstract concept, is dysfunctional today. Hence, a solution to the Kashmir question has to be found *ab initio*, since these UN Resolutions are unimplementable.

All the solutions proposed to date: the plebiscite option, the Line of Control partition, the UN Trusteeship, the Irish model, fall outside one or both of the above-stated parameters and, thus, are not *sustainable* solutions. We have to search for a new alternative solution.

Postscript

Terrorism and Human Rights in the India's Constitutional Framework*

1. Introduction

The Constitution of India is considered a living instrument, one that can be adapted and amended according to socio-economic developments in society within the framework of the Preamble to the Constitution given to us by the Freedom loving peoples of our nation. It contains 447 Articles divided into 26 Parts and 12 Schedules. The Preamble, Part III of the Constitution consisting of Fundamental Rights, Part IV comprising Directive Principles, and Part IV (A) containing Fundamental Duties, constitute the Human Rights framework of our Constitution.[1]

The Preamble part of the Basic Structure of the Constitution[2] sets out the aims and aspirations of the people during the Freedom struggle that have been translated into various provisions of the Constitution.

Thus,Fundamental Rights contained in Part III of the Indian Constitution are enforceable or justiciable rights. This implies that, upon violation or denial of those Rights, a citizen is entitled to the constitutional remedy contained in Article 32. But Constitution

[1] *The Supreme in I.R. Coelho v. State of Tamil Nadu, AIR 2007 SC 861.*

[2] *Kesavananda Bharti v. State of Kerala, AIR 1973 SC1461.*

*This post script had drawn on the publication: *Human Rights and Humanitarian Law of the South Asia Human Rights Documentation Centre, New Delhi, and published by Oxford University Press (2008).*

also mandates Government to impose "Reasonable Restrictions" on Fundamental Rights, even on the Right to Free Speech.

Under Article 368, provisions of the Constitution can be changed or amended or struck downby means of an Amendment. Since it came into effect in 1950, there have been no fewer than 103 Amendments to the Constitution. Terrorism thus has to be combated within the boundaries of 'reasonable restriction' on Fundamental Right in the Constitution. Otherwise than on reasonable restrictions Human Rightsare Fundamental Rights that prevails.

Directive Principles, contained in Part IV of the Constitution, aimed at welfare of citizens based on justice in social, political, and economic life. Article 37 of the Constitution holds these Directive Principles as fundamental for governance of the country and the State *shall apply these principles* in making law.

Fundamental Duties are contained in Part IV A of the Constitution and were added to the Constitution by way of the forty second amendment in 1976. Traditional duties such as protecting the unity and integrity of the country, safe keeping of public property, protection of the environment, etc., which require basic norms of democratic conduct from all citizens, have thus been vested with a constitutional character.

BASIC STRUCTURE DOCTRINE

In *Kesavananda Bharati v. State of Kerala*: The Supreme Court formulated the 'Basic Structure' doctrine, prescribing *limits* on the extent and scope of constitutional amendments under Article 368. The Apex court held 'that the amending power cannot be exercised in a manner as to destroy or emasculate the basic or Fundamental Features of the Constitution'. As the concept of Basic Structure is not found within the Constitution itself, having been introduced by the Supreme Court, there is no enumerated list of those features, and as such it falls to the Supreme Court to judge on a case-by-case basics, whether it is possible to amend a particular Article. In *Kesavananda Bharati case* a preliminary list of features forming part of the Basic Structure of the Constitution was propounded. Later in 1993, the Bommai case judgment, also carried further the list the elements of Basic Structure.

Any amendment to the Constitution must *be tested by the doctrine of Basic Structure*. Any law seeking to amend any fundamental right is subject to the Basic Structure Test. The power of Judicial Review has been construed to form part of the Basic Structure, thus insulating Judicial Review from curtailment by the legislature.

Democracy, Secularism, and Federalism

In *Kiboto Hollohon* case it was held that democracy was a Basic Feature, of which regular, free and fair elections, as well as procedures to resolve disputes over elections were vital components. *This was reaffirmed in Bommai case of 1993.*

Since the introduction of the doctrine of Basic Structure in *Kesavananda Bharati case* in 1973, the Basic Features of the Constitution have been propounded, affirmed, and added to by the Supreme Court in a subsequent series of decisions. The notion that 'certain values and ideals' embedded in the Constitution should be preserved and not destroyed by any process of constitutional amendment has thus been upheld in the judicial process, and the judiciary has respected its obligation to uphold the values of the Indian Constitution.[3]

IMPLEMENTATION OF INTERNATIONAL LAW FOR HUMAN RIGHTS

When, however, there arises a 'conflict of obligations' between the two systemic issues, national judiciaries and legislatures have sought

[3] *Bhagwati, J. in Minerva Mills &Ors. V. Union of India &Ors, 1980 AIR 1789: 1980 SCC (3) 625, http://judis.nic.in/supremecourt/qrydisp.asp?tfnm=4488.*

to harmonise instead of according preference to one issue over the other. This is evidenced in the observation made by Supreme Court Justice H.R. Khanna in his famous minority opinion in A.D.M. Jabalpur v. S. Shukla case[4], wherein he stated:

"Equally well established is the rule of construction that if there be a conflict between the municipal law on one side and the international law or the provisions of any treaty obligations on the other, the courts would give effect to municipal law. If however, two construction of the municipal law are possible, the courts should lean in favour of adopting such construction as would make the provisions of the municipal law to be in harmony with the international on treaty obligations."

Article 51 (1) (c) of the Indian Constitution directs the state to 'foster respect for international law and treaty obligations'. Article 253 vests the Parliament with the power to enact laws to implement treaties ratified by India. Further, under Entry 14 of list I of the Seventh Schedule, the Central Government has exclusive authority to enter into and implement treaties, conventions, and agreements with foreign countries.

The Supreme Court has, however, favoured application of the provisions and principles of international law *in the absence of legislative incorporation.* In *Maganbhai Ishwarbhi Patel v. Union of India*[5] the Supreme Court held:

In other words, if the rights guaranteed by a Treaty are supplementary or similar to those contained in the Indian Constitution and do not in any way impinge or restrict them, no specific legislation is warranted to implement the obligations. The crime of Genocide has now been accepted by the Government's Union Home Ministry vide answers to Rajya Sabha questions, as part of Indian Penal Code.

[4]AIR 1976 SC 1207, http://judis.nic.in/supremecourt/qrydisp.asp?tfnm=5622.
[5](1970) 3 SCC 400.

India thus has favoured a consideration of domestic law, that is in keeping with the state's obligations under an international treaty or convention to which it is a party, especially is cases where the legislation is enacted during or after ratification or entry into force of the international treaty.[6] In *Gramophone Company of India Ltd v. Birendra Bahadur Pandey*,[7] the Apex Court held that while international provisions were construed to have been incorporated within municipal law in the absence of contradiction, in case of conflict 'the sovereignty and the integrity of the Republic and the supremacy of the constituted legislatures in making the laws may not be subjected to external rules except to the extent legitimately accepted by the constituted legislatures themselves.'

In *Jolly George Verghese v. Bank of Cochin*,[8] the Supreme Court of India went further than *Gramophone* and held that while primacy would have to be accorded to national law, "it is a principle generally recognised in national legal system that, in event of doubt, the national rule is to be interpreted in accordance with the State's international obligations."

In the case of *Vishaka v. State of Rajasthan*, the Supreme Court held that, in the absence of domestic law provisions, reliance could be placed on international law as well as international norms that were not in contravention of any existing domestic law and the Constitution. Upholding the nation of gender equality, in the absence of any enacted law to prevent sexual harassment at the workplace, the Court relied heavily upon the provisions of the *UN Convention on the Elimination of All Forms of Discrimination Against Women*. The Court held: 'There is no reason why these international

[6] *Justice Anand, A.S., 'The Domestic Application of International Human Rights Norms', Inaugural Address, at* www.humanrightsinitiative.org/jc/papers/jc_2003/backgroud_papers/BP_Anand.pdf.

[7] *AIR 1984 SC 667,* http://judis.nic.in/supremecourt.qrydisp.asp?tfnm=9599.

[8] *1980 SCR (2) 913.*

conventions and norms cannot, therefore, be used for construing the fundamental rights expressly guaranteed in the Constitution of India which embody the basic concept of gender equality in all spheres of human activity. Further in *Apparel Export Promotion Council v. A.K. Chopra*[9], the Apex Court underlined the 'obligation (of the Court) to see that the message of the international instruments is not allowed to be drowned.'

CIVIL AND POLITICAL RIGHTS

The Indian Constitution, however, reflects the classification of human rights as per Civil and Political rights are contained in Part III (Fundamental Rights) of the Constitution and are justiciable, i.e. they can be enforced through a court of law. Economic, social, and cultural rights are contained in Part IV (Directive Principles of State Policy-DPSPs) and are non-enforceable in a court of law by individuals, aggraded *but are fundamental to governance*'.[10]

Rights to Fundamental Freedoms

Article 19(1) of the Constitution guarantees six fundamental freedoms available to Indian citizens throughout the territory of India. They are as follows:

* freedom of speech and expression [Article 19(1) (a)]
* freedom to assemble peaceably without arms [Article 19(1) (b)]
* freedom to form associations or unions [Article 19(1) (c)]
* freedom of movement [Article 19(1) (d)]
* freedom to reside and settle in any part of India [Article 19(1) (e)]
* freedom to practise any profession or carry on any occupation, trade or business [Article 19(1) (f)]

[9] *(1999) 1 SCC 759,* http://judis.nic.in/supremecourt/qrydisp.asp?tfnm=17025.

[10] *Article 37, Indian Constitution, Article 37 of Directive Principles.*

This cluster of rights is vertical in nature, *enforceable only against the state and its instrumentalities.* None of the rights are absolute, and hence are subject to 'reasonable restrictions' the specific interest of the community as well as of the State. The state can through legislation restrict reasonably the freedoms of Act 19(1) on the basis of grounds in clauses (2) to (6) of Article 19 of the Constitution. These restrictions also seek to circumscribe the extent to which the state can curb the exercise of the fundamental freedoms. The courts will evaluate the validity of restrictions on the basis of a two-fold test – the reasonableness of the restriction and whether it falls within the grounds on the basis of which restrictions can be imposed.

Rights to Life and Personal Liberty

Right to Life

Article 21 of the Constitution guarantees all citizens and non-citizens protections of life and personal liberty. In *Francis Coralie v. Union Territory of Delhi*[11] the Supreme Court interpreted the right to life broadly us:

The Right to Life includes the right to live with human dignity and all that goes along with it, namely, the bare necessities of life such as adequate nutrition, clothing and shelter and facilities for reading, writing and expressing oneself in diverse forms, freely moving about and mixing and commingling with fellow human beings.

The Supreme Court, elaborating in *Ramsharan Autyanuprasi v. Union of India* stated that life is all those things that give meaning to an individual's life, the scope of Article 21 including tradition, heritage and culture, and preservation of the same. The expansive interpretation of Article 21 by the judiciary has lead to the inclusion of several rights within the right to life, *and to speedy justice* to the status of a Fundamental Right.

[11](1981) 1 SCC 608, http://judis.nic.in/supremecourt/qrydisp.asp?tfnm=8118.

Human Rights and Terrorism Law

The Unlawful Activities (Prevention) Amendment Act, 2005

The Unlawful Activities (Prevention) Amendment Act (UAPA) was adopted by Parliament in February 2005. In most regards, UAPA constituted a considerable improvement on safeguards protecting the accused, bringing in line many of its provisions with that of the Criminal Procedure Code. Thus, in democratic India, *there are sufficient safeguards in the Constitution to prevent misuse of the current laws against Terrorism* such as Prevention of Unlawful Acts as amended in 2005.

For example, the period of allowable detention conforms to Section 167(2)(a)of the Code of Criminal Procedure, which stipulates that all arrested persons have to be produced within twenty-four hours. The admissibility of confessions as evidence *was also repealed*, in accordance with the Indian Evidence Act. The reversal of the burden of proof back to the prosecution also appeared to restore a semblance of legitimacy to Indian criminal justice.

Thus, in India the Human Rights and measures against combating Terrorism have been substantially harmonized without twisting either beyond its meaning scope, and effectiveness.

When all is said and done, it must be remembered always the Terrorism is lawless, brutal, and largely unstructured. Hence, to protect citizens in a democratic society, the State must craft its methods to confront and eliminate terrorism within the contradicting objectives of counter-terror effectiveness and human rights.

Such a difficult harmony of objectives requires constant debate in a democratic society.in a nutshell the performance of State's duty of maintaining public order within reasonable restrictions of human rights provided the Constitutional framework.

Appendix

ISI fomenting trouble in India's north-east: US intelligence
23 April 2007
http://www.rediff.com/news/2007/apr/23isi.htm

Pakistan's Inter-Service Intelligence is working with Bangladesh's intelligence agencies to facilitate cooperation between north-east militant groups like United Liberation Front of Asom and other *jihadi* outfits in South Asian regions, besides Tamil rebels in Lanka, a US intelligence service publication *Startfor* has said.

In its latest forecast titled "India: The Islamisation of the Northeast," it observes that there is a growing Islamization in the region — spurred by ISI, and instability in neighbouring Bangladesh which is giving foreign powers (China and Pakistan) a gamut of exploitable secessionist movements to use to prevent India from emerging as a major global player.

Stratfor says there exists a strong nexus between ISI and Bangladesh's intelligence agencies.

There are growing indications, says the report, that these two agencies are working clandestinely in Bangladesh to bring all the north-east-based insurgent outfits and *jihadi* elements under one umbrella.

"The ISI has facilitated cooperation between ULFA and other north-eastern militant outfits; with the LTTE in Sri Lanka, Islamist militant groups in Jammu and Kashmir, Islamist groups in Bangladesh and a growing number of *Al Qaeda*-linked *jihadi* groups operating in the region," it adds.

"ULFA's growing links with Bangladeshi Islamists and *jihadi* elements in the area are increasingly coming to light," the report claims.

The 9 April attack timed with Prime Minister Manmohan Singh's visit to Assam marked the group's first-ever suicide bombing, a tactic that was pioneered by the Tigers and has been frequently employed by Islamist militants.

ULFA's adoption of suicide bombing, Stratfor says, looks to be the result of the group's increased Islamization caused by collusion with Islamist outfits in the region.

The bomber in the 9 April suicide attack was Ainul Ali. Citing Indian security sources, the report says ULFA did not have many Muslim cadres in its fold in the past, but the increasing flow of Bangladeshi refugees across the border has given the group more—and more capable—members willing to sacrifice their lives for the group's cause with nudging from the ISI, Pakistan's premier intelligence agency.

Political conditions in Bangladesh, observes the report, appear to be indirectly contributing to the empowerment of Islamists there.

Using the Pakistani military regime as an example, Bangladeshi Army chief Lt Gen Moeen U Ahmed is reasserting the army's role in Bangladeshi politics—which have long suffered from a bitter political feud between Awami League, led by Sheikh Hasina, and the Bangladesh Nationalist Party, led by Begum Khaleda Zia, it said.

With both party leaders driven into exile, a political vacuum has started to take root in the country, and Bangladesh's Islamist parties are anxiously waiting to fill it, the report adds.

As a result, it forecasts, New Delhi is facing a "bleak situation" in which the ISI's manoeuvres and Bangladesh's political troubles are sure to further constrain India's ability to dig itself out of the militant trap Pakistan has set for India with the help of Bangladesh.

It quoted one informed Bangladesh observer as saying there does exist meaningful cooperation between ISI and Bangladesh's intelligence agencies in their combined fight against terrorism, at the nudging of the West, but their joint efforts to trap India may just be a collateral strategic gain.

Bibliography

Ambedkar, B.R., "Castes in India: Their Genesis, Mechanism, and developments," *Indian Antiquary,* Vol. XVI, May 1917, p. 94.

Bansel, Alok, "Alienation in Northern Areas of PoK," IDSA Papers, New Delhi (2006).

Byman, Daniel, *Deadly Connections: States That Sponsor Terrorism* (Cambridge University Press, 2007).

Burgees, Mark, *Terrorism: The Problem of Definition*, Centre for Defence Information, Washington D.C., August 2003.

Clive, Ray and Yonsh Alexander, *Terrorism—The Soviet Connection,* Crane Russak, New York, 1984.

Cohen, Stephen, *Idea of Pakistan,* Brookings Institutions, Washington D.C. (2005).

Elst, Koenoraad, *Negationism in India: Concealing the Record of Islam* (Voice of India, 1992) http://koenraadelst.bharatvani.org/books/negaind/index.htm.

George, Alexander L. and Richard Smoke, *Deterrence in American Foreign Policy: Theory and Practice,* Columbia University Press, New York, 1974.

Habeck, Mary, *Knowing the Enemy: Jihadist Ideology and the War on Terror* (Yale University Press, 2006), pp. 42-43.

Habeck, Mary, *Knowing the Enemy: Jihadist Ideology and the War on Terror* (Yale University Press, 2006), p. 17.

Huntington, Samuel, *Who Are We? The Identity of Americans,* Harvard University Press, (2003).

Jones, Owen B, *Pakistan: Eye of the Storm,* Penguin Viking, U.K. (2004).

Krishnappa, Wg. Cdr. V., "Compellence: What is it?" IDSA Draft Papers, (2006).

Misra, Ashutosh, *Jihadi Influence in the Pakistani Army*, IDSA Draft Paper, 19 May 2006.

Mir, Hamid, "We can Hit any Soft Target in India," *Rediff.com*, 9 January 2007, http://ushome.rediff.com/news/2007/jan/09inter.htm.

Muthuswamy, Moorthy, "A New Paradigm for the War on Terror," *The Washington Times*, 8 December 2003.

Pape, Robert, *Dying to Win: The Strategic Logic of Suicide Terrorism*, Random House, (2007).

Schifferdecker, Arnie, "The Taliban-Bin Laden-ISI Connection, *American Foreign Service Association*, 1 December 2002, http://www.asfa.org/fsi/Dec01/Schiff.cfm.

Schwartz, Stephen, "Ground Zero and the Saudi Connection, *The Spectator*, 22 September 2001.

T. K. Singh, "Terror Trends," *Strategic Analysis*, IDSA, New Delhi, September 2006.

Stern, J., *The Ultimate Terrorist*, Harvard University Press (1999), Cambridge, Mass USA.

Swamy, Subramanian, *Hindus Under Siege: The Way Out*, Har-Anand Publications, (2006).

Swamy, Subramanian, *Sri Lanka in Crisis: India's Options*, Har-Anand Publications, 2007.

Trager, Robert and Desseslava Zagorcheva, "Deterring Terrorism—It can be Done," *International Security Journal*, Harvard-MIT, Vol. 30, No. 3, 2006.

The Islamic Trilogy: Volume 2, *The Political Traditions of Mohammed: The Hadith for the Unbelievers* (Centre for the Study of Political Islam, 2006).

Warner, William, "An Ethical Basis for the War Against Political Islam," *Centre for the Study of Political Islam*, 2006, p. 13.

Warner, William, "The Study of Political Islam," *FrontPage Magazine*, 5 February 2007, http://www.frontpagemag.com/Articles/Read Article.asp? ID = 26769